Dangerous Measures

MW01273796

THE AZRIELI SERIES OF HOLOCAUST SURVIVOR MEMOIRS:
PUBLISHED TITLES

ENGLISH TITLES

Dangerous Measures
Joseph Schwarzberg

FIRST EDITION

Copyright © 2018 The Azrieli Foundation and others

All rights reserved

Copyright in individual works, parts of works and/or photographs included within this published work is also claimed by individuals and entities. All requests and questions concerning copyright and reproduction of all or part of this publication may be directed to The Azrieli Foundation.

THE AZRIELI FOUNDATION
www.azrielifoundation.org

Cover and book design by Mark Goldstein
Endpaper maps by Martin Gilbert
Map on page xxxvii by François Blanc
Images of documents courtesy of Yad Vashem.

LIBRARY AND ARCHIVES CANADA CATALOGUING IN PUBLICATION

Schwarzberg, Joseph, 1926–, author
    Dangerous Measures/ Joseph Schwarzberg.

(Azrieli series of Holocaust survivor memoirs. Series x)
Includes bibliographical references and index.
ISBN 978-1-988065-45-8 (softcover) · 8 7 6 5 4 3 2 1

1. Schwarzberg, Joseph, 1926–. 2. Holocaust survivors — Germany — Leipzig — Biography. 3. Holocaust, Jewish (1939–1945) — Germany — Leipzig — Personal narratives. 4. World War, 1939–1945 — Jewish resistance. 5. Autobiographies. I. Azrieli Foundation, issuing body II. Title. III. Series: Azrieli series of Holocaust survivor memoirs. Series x

DS134.42.S39A3 2018   940.53'18092   C2018-905115-9

The Azrieli Series of Holocaust Survivor Memoirs

Naomi Azrieli, Publisher

Jody Spiegel, Program Director
Arielle Berger, Managing Editor
Matt Carrington, Editor
Devora Levin, Assistant Editor
Elizabeth Lasserre, Senior Editor, French-Language Editions
Elin Beaumont, Senior Education Outreach and Program Facilitator
Catherine Person, Bilingual Education and Outreach Coordinator
Stephanie Corazza, Education and Curriculum Associate
Marc-Olivier Cloutier, Bilingual Educational Outreach and Events
    Assistant
Elizabeth Banks, Digital Asset Curator and Archivist
Susan Roitman, Office Manager (Toronto)
Mary Mellas, Executive Assistant and Human Resources (Montreal)

Mark Goldstein, Art Director
François Blanc, Cartographer
Bruno Paradis, Layout, French-Language Editions

Contents

Series Preface:
In their own words...

In telling these stories, the writers have liberated themselves. For so many years we did not speak about it, even when we became free people living in a free society. Now, when at last we are writing about what happened to us in this dark period of history, knowing that our stories will be read and live on, it is possible for us to feel truly free. These unique historical documents put a face on what was lost, and allow readers to grasp the enormity of what happened to six million Jews — one story at a time.

David J. Azrieli, C.M., C.Q., M.Arch
Holocaust survivor and founder, The Azrieli Foundation

Since the end of World War II, approximately 40,000 Jewish Holocaust survivors have immigrated to Canada. Who they are, where they came from, what they experienced and how they built new lives for themselves and their families are important parts of our Canadian heritage. The Azrieli Foundation's Holocaust Survivor Memoirs Program was established in 2005 to preserve and share the memoirs written by those who survived the twentieth-century Nazi genocide of the Jews of Europe and later made their way to Canada. The program is guided by the conviction that each survivor of the Holocaust has a remarkable story to tell, and that such stories play an important role in education about tolerance and diversity.

Millions of individual stories are lost to us forever. By preserving the stories written by survivors and making them widely available to a broad audience, the Azrieli Foundation's Holocaust Survivor Memoirs Program seeks to sustain the memory of all those who perished at the hands of hatred, abetted by indifference and apathy. The personal accounts of those who survived against all odds are as different as the people who wrote them, but all demonstrate the courage, strength, wit and luck that it took to prevail and survive in such terrible adversity. The memoirs are also moving tributes to people — strangers and friends — who risked their lives to help others, and who, through acts of kindness and decency in the darkest of moments, frequently helped the persecuted maintain faith in humanity and courage to endure. These accounts offer inspiration to all, as does the survivors' desire to share their experiences so that new generations can learn from them.

The Holocaust Survivor Memoirs Program collects, archives and publishes select survivor memoirs and makes the print editions available free of charge to educational institutions and Holocaust-education programs across Canada. They are also available for sale to the general public at bookstores. All revenues to the Azrieli Foundation from the sales of the Azrieli Series of Holocaust Survivor Memoirs go toward the publishing and educational work of the memoirs program.

~

The Azrieli Foundation would like to express appreciation to the following people for their invaluable efforts in producing this book: Doris Bergen, Sherry Dodson (Maracle Inc), Farla Klaiman, Therese Parent, Jane Pavanel, and Margie Wolfe & Emma Rodgers of Second Story Press.

About the Glossary

The following memoir contains a number of terms, concepts and historical references that may be unfamiliar to the reader. For information on major organizations; significant historical events and people; geographical locations; religious and cultural terms; and foreign-language words and expressions that will help give context and background to the events described in the text, please see the glossary beginning on page 153.

Introduction

Leipzig, Brussels, Paris, Southern France, Israel: an itinerary that is emblematic of the geographical wanderings of many Jews in the twentieth century. Rising antisemitism in Germany, escape to a safer country, the turmoil of World War II and, finally, the creation of a new country, are all stages in Joseph Schwarzberg's life, and his memoir vividly illustrates this slice of history.

From Leipzig to France through Belgium

Joseph, born in Leipzig in 1926, was six years old when Adolf Hitler was appointed chancellor of Germany by Paul von Hindenburg, the president, on January 30, 1933, after a series of parliamentary elections. He was a child. However, like other Jewish children of that era, he was quickly confronted with a reality that did not leave much space for a carefree childhood.

At that time, the Jews in Germany comprised less than 1 per cent of the population. Out of the 525,000 Jews in the country, approximately 12,000 were living in Leipzig, while the total population of the city amounted roughly to half a million people. Joseph was one of the 60,000 school-aged Jewish children (between the ages of six and fourteen) in Germany.

The history of the Jewish community in Leipzig followed a path that distinguished it from other Jewish communities in Germany. In 1543, Duke Maurice of Saxony expelled all Jews from his dominions. From that point until the unification of Germany and the formation of the German Reich in 1871, the Jewish presence in Leipzig was linked to the developing fur industry and, more specifically, to the fairs that were held there every year at Easter. Jews from the Polish provinces, which had been annexed by Russia, Prussia and Austria at the end of the eighteenth century, dominated this trade and came in increasing numbers to attend the fairs. As *Ostjuden*, immigrant Jews of Eastern European origin, they were merely tolerated and were refused the right to settle permanently in the city and denied naturalization by the antisemitic Saxon state. The most well-known example is probably that of Jacob Freud, Sigmund Freud's father, who applied (three times) for a permanent residence permit in Leipzig during his 1859 visit to the fair — an application that was ultimately rejected. As a result, in the autumn of that same year, the family moved to Vienna, where little Sigmund would become so famous.

After the emancipation, which came around the time of the unification of Germany, the German authorities began granting citizenship certificates more liberally, and the Jewish community of Leipzig doubled over the next twenty years, reaching more than six thousand members. The majority of the newcomers were from Eastern Europe. Yet, this liberality did not last long under a growing antisemitic sentiment, and naturalization almost ceased to be granted. At the beginning of the twentieth century, new waves of Jewish immigrants from the same areas arrived in Leipzig in the wake of several events: the first Russian pogroms, the economic depression in Austria's Polish provinces (particularly Galicia), the 1917 Russian Revolution, and the dissolution of the Austro-Hungarian Empire and resurrection of the Polish state at the end of World War I. By the beginning of the 1930s, the Jewish population of Leipzig had doubled again. Made up mostly of immigrants from Eastern Europe (some of whom came to Leipzig as Austrian nationals and were suddenly attached to the new Polish state or became "stateless") in a state that denied them citizenship, the Jewish community of Leipzig had a singular place among German-Jewish communities. The German-Jewish population of Leipzig was not more than 30 per cent of the whole Jewish community; 70 per cent of the Jews were from other countries and were referred to as "foreigners" — most of them were Polish or stateless. In other German cities, the numbers were reversed: an average of 70 per cent of the Jews had German citizenship. Leipzig was therefore the German city with the largest number of Eastern Jews after Berlin and as a consequence, perhaps, a centre for antisemitic propaganda. Zionism, in its varied forms, provided many Jews in Leipzig with a rhetorical home, but the Jewish community there was one of the most varied and sometimes divided in the country.

Immediately after the Nazis assumed power, the Third Reich initiated a legislative assault on Jews that shattered the foundations of the Jewish community. On April 1, 1933, the regime declared a national boycott of Jewish businesses as "a defensive measure" against anti-Nazi propaganda abroad, for which Jews were blamed. In September 1935, the Nuremberg Laws were enacted, establishing racial segregation between Jews and non-Jews. Jews lost their rights as citizens. From then on, as Professor Marion Kaplan has put it, "For Jews, daily fear was accompanied by economic strangulation."[1] By the mid-1930s, Jews were completely isolated from the rest of the population. They were gradually excluded from employment, and non-German Jews even had to leave jobs within Jewish institutions. The impact of these measures was especially felt in Leipzig, given its high percentage of non-German Jews.

Children were not spared. In April 1933, the Law against the Overcrowding of German Schools established a *numerus clausus* that

---

1   Marion Kaplan, *Between Dignity and Despair: Jewish Life in Nazi Germany*. (New York: Oxford University Press, 1999), 11.

meant only 1.5 per cent of students in German schools were allowed to be Jews. As a consequence, many families enrolled their children in Jewish schools, changing the percentage of Jewish children who attended — from 14 per cent in 1932 to 60 per cent in 1937.

This was a time of segregation and exclusion, but the Nazi regime did not stop there. On October 27 and 28, Germany expelled 17,000 Polish Jews to the Polish border. They were denied entry and found themselves in a no-man's land, with neither food nor shelter. The number of Jewish victims of this expulsion from Leipzig is not clear; estimates put it between 1,600 and 3,500.

The worst was yet to come. During the night of November 9, 1938, and the following day, Germany was the scene of a violent pogrom initiated by the highest authorities in the state. Close to two hundred synagogues and places of worship were burned, 7,500 Jewish businesses were wrecked, some hundred Jews were brutally killed, several hundred were wounded or committed suicide and close to 30,000 Jews were deported to the camps of Dachau, Buchenwald and Sachsenhausen. Altogether, between 2,000 and 2,500 Jews met their death in Germany as a result of the night that would become known as Kristallnacht.

Emigration from Nazi Germany became a priority for every Jew after the November pogrom. But it was far from easy: how could one get exit and entry permits when bureaucratic and financial conditions imposed by the Nazi regime made the former laborious, and immigration restrictions in foreign countries forbade the acquisition of the latter? Marion Kaplan quotes the German-Jewish journalist Bella Fromm to illustrate "the plight of all German Jews": "So far, I have gathered a collection of twenty-three of the necessary documents. I have made a thorough study of the employees and furniture in fifteen official bureaus...during the hours I have waited."[2] And yet, some documents were still missing.

---

2 Ibid., 130.

Around seventy-eight thousand Jews fled from Germany in the first year following Kristallnacht. By September 1939, about two thirds of the Jewish community had left Germany. After the expulsion of Polish Jews and Kristallnacht, emigration became the highest priority for Leipzig Jews, too. The foreigners were the most eager to leave. But the obstacles preventing legal emigration drove a number of Jews, there as in the rest of Germany, to opt for clandestine routes, which led them to Belgium or France.

This was the case with the Schwarzberg family. They were of Polish origin and kept close ties with their siblings who remained in Poland. Joseph joined a Zionist youth group and followed with enthusiasm the accomplishments of the nascent Jewish community (the Yishuv) in Palestine. Yet, his family seemed to favour integration into German society, until this became impossible: they did not live in a Jewish neighbourhood, their son went to a German school where he was surrounded by non-Jewish pupils, many customers for whom Joseph's parents sewed clothes were German non-Jews. At the same time, their closest friends were Jews. This illustration of the complexity of Jewish life in Germany runs counter to simplistic views of Jewish identity in Western countries at that time. But enduring exclusion resonated differently depending on whether you were born German, had immigrated to Germany a while ago or had just arrived in the country. In that respect, accompanying Joseph as he describes the daily life of a Jewish family with a distinct identity but in a mixed neighbourhood, at a time when the Nazis were extending their grip on German society, is particularly enlightening. It is clear how important the solidarity of the Jewish community was in getting through the growing persecution, as were friendly connections with non-Jews.

Even more so, this memoir allows us to follow the gradual and yet rapid exclusion of Jews from German society through the eyes of a child. The anti-Jewish laws and the increasing antisemitic propaganda become concrete realities as they translate into the everyday life of a German-Jewish child. Joseph felt the anxiety of the adults, paid close attention to multiple reasons given for why Hitler would never come to power, felt excluded from the national narrative — which gained in importance and took over each and every aspect of life — and experienced the coexistence of two parallel realities: a normal one in which things seemed to be unchanged, and another one in which the normality of yesterday was continuously vanishing. True, his parents could go on working with their regular Christian clients for a while, but antisemitic propaganda was pouring through the media and could not help but turn his life upside down.

At the age of ten, Joseph's inner world was shaped for life: his political awareness was awakened through discussions among adults about the Spanish Civil War; he had to transfer from a German school to a Jewish one and from one neighbourhood to another; and he felt suddenly estranged from the whole of society, which had been his own only a little while earlier. Joseph did not live a regular childhood, and the little anecdotes he records allow us to grasp this reality much better than any objective description could have.

The Schwarzbergs, like many German families, had to split up in order to leave Germany. Joseph's father left for Belgium first and was held there in a camp for illegal immigrants. Joseph describes how he and his six-year-old sister were smuggled through the border. Having only enough money to pay for smugglers for them, their mother met them in Belgium one week later, having crossed the border on her own. The story of their time in Brussels is similar to that of many Jewish families: they received help from local Jewish organizations, and as refugees they were estranged from the local Jewish community. But the transnational experience of this young refugee in his new milieu, mingling with Jews who fled from so many countries, is particularly well depicted: "A colourful mix of people gathered there, making for a practical education in diversity, and I learned the customs and dialects of people from all over Europe, including Austria, southern Europe, Czechoslovakia, Hungary, Romania and the Balkans."

When the war stopped being a threat only and became a harsh reality, the idea that it would not last and that Germany would quickly
be defeated dominated for a while. But soon it became evident to the
refugees that it was necessary to move again. There was a mass exodus — by train, by foot, by every possible means — of tens of thousands of refugees travelling toward the south under German bombs,
while the enemy troops were progressing. Twenty thousand Jews, one
third of the Jews living in Belgium at the time, were among these
refugees, as was the Schwarzberg family. The majority of those who
left returned to Belgium once the military front was stabilized.

There are very few recorded descriptions of this mass flight from
Brussels to France and back, and Joseph's memoir provides important
details about his and his family's life during that time. For him this
period meant becoming an adult, not so much as a result of his age,
but because of the precariousness of being a refugee family.

After the May 1940 invasion, Belgium was considered of great
military importance to the Germans and came under direct German
military control. The anti-Jewish policy was to follow at the end of
October 1940. By the end of 1941, as in all of Western Europe, the Jews
of Belgium had to submit to a census. They were then robbed of their
possessions by agents of the German government, and a local council
of Jews was established. The Germans soon attained their objective:
Jews were stripped of all their rights and eliminated from the public,
economic, cultural and social life of the country.

In November 1941, concerned about the reaction of the local
population when native Belgian Jews would be subjected to deportation, the German authorities began denationalizing all Reich Jews
living abroad, transforming them into stateless refugees. This could
facilitate the enactment of the upcoming deportation policy by creating categories of groups to be sent to the east, according to priority.
In early June 1942, the new phase in the anti-Jewish policy could be
launched, with the decree of the yellow Star of David, which inaugurated the implementation of the Final Solution in Western Europe.

Everything was in place to deport the Jews from these countries and send them to the death camps.

This is when Joseph left Belgium for France again, alone this time, as he "erroneously considered Pétain's Vichy France to be free." From what he had witnessed in Germany, he had a feeling that the yellow star was only a beginning, and his family did not comply with the yellow star decree. He began using false papers, which had become relatively easy to obtain thanks to the activities of different resistance organizations in Brussels, Jewish as well as non-Jewish. While hiding in Brussels with some Spanish smugglers, he got their help crossing the border to France. For this sixteen-year-old, it was the start of a journey that would lead to him joining the French Resistance.

In Vichy France

The image of France that young Joseph had in his mind when he crossed the border from Belgium was far from accurate. On June 22, 1940, after its shocking and amazingly swift defeat at the hands of the German army — in which 92,000 soldiers were killed, over 200,000 were wounded, and over 1.5 million French people were taken as prisoners of war — France accepted the terms of an armistice that dismantled the country and paved the way for the end of the Third Republic. The eastern provinces (Alsace and Moselle) were torn away; the Germans occupied the capital as well as the northern part of the country, which was also the richest in terms of natural resources. A new order, the French State (*l'État français*), replaced the republic that had been severely criticized during the 1930s and was now blamed for the disaster.

The Germans imposed decree after decree in Paris and throughout the occupied zone; Marshal Henri Philippe Pétain and his government in Vichy retained sovereignty over less than half of French territory — the so-called free zone. A demarcation line separated the northern occupied area of the country and the southern Vichy-controlled area.

Until March 1943, the only possible way to cross this line legally was to obtain an *Ausweis*, an authorization to travel from one zone to another, from the German military authorities; for Jews, the crossing was absolutely forbidden during all the years of occupation. French gendarmes on the southern side worked hard to catch refugees who succeeded in illegally crossing the demarcation line and put them in refugee camps.

Xenophobia and antisemitism found their way into the measures adopted by the Pétain government as part of the "national revolution" and were applied throughout the country. This arrangement sought to put the country back on its feet and restore its status in the new Europe that was emerging in the shadow of the Third Reich, with which the new regime collaborated actively.

The Jews of the occupied zone soon found themselves victimized by dual antisemitic legislation, German and French. On September 27, 1940, the Germans ordered a census of all Jews and required the French police to stamp Jews' identity papers so that they could be identified at all checkpoints. For its part, the Vichy government inaugurated its antisemitic policy with a series of measures that denaturalized foreigners who had acquired French citizenship during the preceding decades and limited access to certain professions to native-born French citizens. Next, the Jewish Statute, issued on October 3, 1940, transformed the Jews into second-class citizens overnight, banishing them from the civil service, officer ranks and all fields that influenced public opinion, such as communications, movies and journalism. On October 4, 1940, the regime issued an edict that authorized prefects to intern foreign Jews in special camps by administrative order. This decree made it possible to send forty thousand foreign Jews to camps in the so-called free zone. It also served as the legal basis for the roundups there, as well as in Paris, where it led to the internment of some eight thousand Jews in 1941 alone. When making these arrests, the French police used lists drawn up from the registry of Jews created by police headquarters, working off the Jewish census of September 1940. Anxious to retain or recover its sovereignty — its main obsession — in as many domains as possible, the Vichy government placed its bureaucracy at the disposal of the German occupier in the northern zone to enforce the anti-Jewish regulations that confined Jews to a social and cultural ghetto. It also seized Jewish property in a progressive wave of confiscations mandated by the German occupation authorities in order to "Aryanize" the economy.

The antisemitic legislation was completed with a new Jewish Statute issued on June 2, 1941. This law enlarged the definition of who was to be considered a Jew, purged Jews from the liberal professions, extended the list of occupations from which they were excluded and instituted a *numerus clausus* of 3 per cent in the universities. It also called for a Jewish census in the Vichy zone and the "Aryanization" of Jewish property.

Ostracism and dispossession were merely preliminary stages. Starting in the spring of 1942, the application of the Final Solution to the Jews of France became the order of the day. But it was the appearance of the yellow star in the streets of Paris and throughout the occupied zone that clearly indicated the magnitude of the change. Exactly at the same time as in Belgium, the Eighth Ordinance from the German military command in France, signed on May 29, 1942, and published on June 1, required Jews over the age of six to permanently affix to their clothes a six-pointed yellow star with black borders, which had to be the size of the palm of the hand.

But even those measures were only a prelude. Arrest followed by deportation to an unknown destination became the most terrifying threat to the Jewish population, first in the occupied zone and then throughout the country. Three convoys set out for Auschwitz from the camps in the occupied zone on June 22, 25 and 28, 1942. These camps, emptied of their inmates, could now absorb new victims.

On July 16 and 17, 1942, and over the following days, 13,152 stateless Jews, including 5,919 women and 4,115 children, were arrested in

Paris by the French police as part of a vast operation that came to be known as the Vel d'Hiv Roundup. The families were sent first to the Vélodrome d'Hiver and then to the infamous Drancy camp, before their final journey to Auschwitz in sealed freight cars.

In early August, the Jews of the southern zone suddenly faced the same threat. The internment camps and camps for foreign workers there provided new cargo for the sealed freight cars that rumbled toward the death camps. Then, everywhere in what was still called the free zone, French police arrested foreign Jews, using census lists that had already been drawn up.

The mass arrests of Jews conducted by the French police continued in waves throughout both zones until February 1944. There were also the constant arrests of individuals, an activity in which the German police, aided by auxiliary forces drawn from French collaborationist groups, were increasingly involved. After November 1942, when the Germans took control of the southern zone following the Allied landing in North Africa, the occupation authorities operated throughout French territory. The arrests of Jews continued until the liberation of the entire country. Moreover, the circle of potential victims kept expanding: Jews of foreign nationality; French Jews; those in possession of a German-issued *Ausweis,* which had formerly granted them a measure of protection; activists of recognized and legal Jewish organizations; hospital patients and residents of senior-citizens' homes; and finally, children. No Jew was safe. All told, almost seventy-six thousand Jews were deported from France, of whom only 3 per cent survived.

When Joseph arrived in Paris, he was not identified as a Jew and did not wear the yellow star. His discovery of places he had only heard about until then is touching and probably took him far away from the harsh reality of being a refugee and a foreigner in the city. The magic of the city of lights, even during the German occupation, combined harmoniously with the magic of youth — a touching passage in Joseph's memoir.

Paradoxically, before the deportations to the camps in the east began, more Jews and foreigners were prisoners in internment camps in the free zone then in the occupied one. All kinds of initiatives by Jewish and non-Jewish charitable organizations were launched to try to either help the Jewish internees in the camps, where the conditions were absolutely awful, or to liberate them from behind barbed wire.

Abbot Glasberg, vicar of Notre-Dame de Saint-Alban in Lyon, was the driving force of one of the initiatives aimed at freeing at least some of the internees. Born a Jew in the Ukraine, Alexandre Glasberg immigrated to France in 1931. He converted to Catholicism and was ordained as a priest in 1938. Over the course of the first few months of 1941, Abbot Glasberg, Nina Gourfinkel (who was then heading a committee in charge of helping refugees) and Doctor Joseph Weill (a central figure in the O S E, Oeuvre de Secours aux Enfants, which was active in the internment camps and later in the rescue of Jewish children) founded the Main Office for the Shelters (D C A), which was to take in foreign Jews released from the camps. They obtained the support of Cardinal Pierre-Marie Gerlier, the Archbishop of Lyon and Primate of Gaul, and then, on June 13, 1941, received authorization from the Ministry of the Interior, which specified clearly that this was a transfer — not to be confused with a release — and that the internees could not stray more than five kilometres from their shelter.

On November 25, 1941, the first group of internees was allowed out of the Gurs internment camp. Shelters were created, and one third of those released paid for everyone in the group: the shelters thus maintained financial self-sufficiency. According to Nina Gourfinkel, about a thousand people, two-thirds of whom were Jewish, stayed in these shelters at one time or another. Since Abbot Glasberg was working outside of official Vichy channels with the support of the most prominent figure of the Catholic hierarchy, he succeeded, at least partially, where others had failed. Eight per cent of those who were released found their way into one of Abbot Glasberg's homes.

During police roundups, Glasberg would use his influence to

limit the application of the new measures against Jews, and to various degrees, resorted to illegal channels. He was then at the head of
an ecumenical organization, Amitié Chrétienne, which, during the
1942 roundups, focused its activities on trying to save Jews, hand in
hand with Jewish organizations. The Château du Bégué in Cazaubon
(Gers), the third of the DCA shelters, was probably created in August 1942. The director was Abbot Glasberg's brother, Victor Vermont
(Vila Glasberg), until he was arrested on August 16, 1943. The Château du Bégué quickly transformed into a shelter for refugees who
had escaped from the occupied zone as well as for young men who
refused to be sent to work in Germany, thus disobeying the Vichy
government's decision (February 1943).

Joseph's memoir provides a unique account of life in Château du
Bégué: he describes the diversity of the refugees who were sheltered
there, the internal organization of the château and the connections
that were established with the surrounding population. Reading his
story, we understand better how social workers, active in helping refugees who were fleeing persecution, turned to resistance work, either
in the form of clandestinely organized rescue operations or through
armed activity.

By November 1942, the situation in the southern zone had
changed. As a consequence of the Allied landing in North Africa, the
German troops invaded what could no longer be labelled the "free
zone," and arrests of Jews increased as Germans took more direct
control of the police work. At this point, the reaction of the French
population shifted from acceptance to hostility. Until the imposition
of the yellow star on the Jews in the occupied zone, the vast majority
of the French people, traumatized by the crushing defeat, placed their
hopes in Marshal Pétain, the charismatic hero of Verdun. This meant
supporting the measures he deemed necessary to restore France, including the antisemitic legislation that seemed to address a problem
widely discussed in the 1930s, the "Jewish problem," and which might
be put as follows: The Jews constituted a distinct social group with

identifiable characteristics. They were naturally bound to the Jews of foreign countries — thus local and foreign Jews were lumped together. They were attracted by money and power and tended to stick together and help one another. They were attracted to subversive ideas. Their presence was disproportionate in certain fields — the press, politics, finance or the film industry, where they asserted their power. Therefore, it was only normal that the French people took offense, especially when the arrival of refugees augmented the power of the Jews. The Vichy legislation seemed to be an attempt to provide a solution to this problem, which was deemed a threat to French society.

All the same, in the occupied zone, anti-Jewish measures that bore the German brand — such as the placarding of Jewish-owned shops — were often viewed with hostility because the general public, although it found a way to adapt to the German presence, viewed the occupiers in a negative light. In the southern zone, by contrast, it was the French State that applied anti-Jewish legislation, and this endowed the discriminatory edicts with a strong measure of legitimacy.

This remained true until the summer of 1942, when an about-turn took place: the first appearance of yellow stars on the streets of Paris and then the sight of the mass roundups of Jews provoked an outburst of indignation. The star and the roundups were no longer expressions of a traditional and long-consecrated French antisemitism, but of French submission to methods deemed barbarous and imposed by a country considered to be barbaric.

From this time on, the evolution of public opinion about various aspects of the antisemitic policy was intrinsically linked to its change in attitude toward Vichy and the Germans, which in turn largely depended on the military situation and expectations as to the outcome of the war. Since the roundups of the summer of 1942, the policy of persecution was closely associated with the occupier. When the German troops occupied the southern zone, the illusion of a Free France collapsed. During 1943, the outcome of the war became clear: an Allied victory was only a matter of time. This further highlighted the illegitimacy of the Vichy government as it sank deeper and deeper into collaboration with the Germans.

As a result of Germany's order for young French men to do forced labour in Germany, an alternative society was emerging gradually in France, and the Jews found it easier to locate allies to help them escape the roundups. The change was perceptible at all levels. There were places where the local population was actively complicit in helping the Jews, especially in regions with a Huguenot (Protestant) majority. But even elsewhere Jews were often able to live quietly without being denounced by their neighbours. As the gulf widened between the French people and the French State, some agencies of the latter lost their effectiveness because their officials had to consider the attitudes of the population they were dealing with. Parallel to this development, some groups of French fascists and ultra-collaborationists, who pushed for closer harmonization between the French regime's politics and the Nazi regime's objectives, increased the number and violence of their actions against resistance activists as well as against Jews.

Resistance

Joseph became active in a resistance organization after he left the château. Resistance, for him as for others, began with small acts. Many French people, and even more so the Jews who had been excluded from a large variety of jobs, had no choice but to work in industries that provided goods for the Germans. In these situations, individual and random acts of sabotage sometimes paved the way for more involved resistance activity. Joseph's account is of particular importance, as it highlights the links between Jewish and non-Jewish structures in the French Resistance. There were numerous Jews in the different resistance movements formed in France, as well as in London around General de Gaulle. But there were also specifically Jewish groups, some of which had been created under the aegis of the French Communist Party, while Zionist groups and Jewish so-cial organizations specialized in the rescue of Jews threatened with deportation.

Yet the enrolment of many Jews in the Communist organizations was not always related to their politics. The French Communist Party had been very active among immigrants before the war, and in or-der to facilitate the dissemination of the Party's ideas and policies among them, it had created, in 1926, a specific organization, the MOE (Main d'œuvre étrangère), which six years later would become the MOI (Main d'œuvre immigrée). A police report mentions the found-ing meeting of a working group of Jewish Communists as early as July 1, 1927.

In the pre-war years, twelve language sections of the French Com-munist Party experienced major growth (especially under the Popu-lar Front). The Jewish section (the Yiddish-language group) was one of the most dynamic. The Molotov-Ribbentrop pact (August 23, 1939) led to the dissolution of the Party in France and triggered a policy of repression that the Vichy regime intensified. Therefore, all Com-munist activity became clandestine even before the fighting began. The German offensive against the Soviet Union, launched on June 22, 1941, simplified the Party's propaganda efforts. Its influence with the population increased, and it gradually found legitimacy in French political society. This legitimacy rested on two elements — anti-Ger-man political activism and the scope of the repression, which merged the image of the hero with that of a victim. The Communist activists were the first to engage in bold military actions (through the Organ-isation Spéciale and then the Francs-Tireurs et Partisans [FTP]), and throughout the war they remained the most active armed resisters.

While the war went on, the victories of the Red Army reversed the French perception of Stalin and the Soviet Union, with the turn-ing point being the victory at Stalingrad. The Communist Party's image as the leader of all the resisting forces was reinforced when it created large organizations (Front organizations) that were not

officially recognized as Communist, in order to recruit widely among
the French population and gradually gain its support of the Party's
politics. The other French movements active in the Resistance could
not ignore this development, and a collaboration between the different ideological currents was established, with the active support of
the Free French Forces in London. While the landing on the beaches
of Normandy was approaching and during the battles for liberation,
the BBC in London was broadcasting coded instructions to all the
groups active in France. This coordination between the Allies and the
resistance movements in France considerably shortened the fight for
the liberation of the country during the summer of 1944.

The Jewish Communists of the MOI, working under the Party's
authority, introduced its policy to the Jewish community in France.
Young Jews were soon playing an active role in the underground
Communist group Organisation Spéciale (which specialized in sabotage), even before the organized military units of the FTP-MOI were
set up in the spring of 1942. Jews who followed this path — many of
them veterans of the International Brigades who had cut their teeth
in Spain — were a minority of the Jewish Communists active in these
groups, which found it difficult to comply with the Party directive
that organizations should send 10 per cent of their membership to
the FTP fighting units. But they accounted for 90 per cent of the first
FTP-MOI unit, composed of Romanians and Hungarians, and the
entire second unit — the Jewish unit — of the four units set up. What
is more, there was a group composed exclusively of Jewish women
who, under the orders of a central logistics department, transported
arms intended for the various units. Finally, the intelligence service
that drew up the plans for all these actions was also staffed by Jewish
women of the MOI.

The Party leadership had made a somewhat astonishing decision.
Since the beginning of 1942, young Jewish Communists, previously
found throughout the organization, had been concentrated in special
units, even though they were French and fully integrated into French

society. This primarily affected the children of immigrant families. But young French Jews who — by a chance encounter or through a relative — joined the ranks of a Communist organization were often directed to a specifically Jewish unit or group. There is no doubt that this facilitated the recruitment of new members. The Union de la jeunesse juive (UJJ), in which Joseph became active, was the front organization created by the MOI in order to recruit young Jews who were eager to resist occupation, whatever their ideological beliefs.

The Jewish unit was the first FTP-MOI unit to go into action. They became the vanguard of military action, first in the capital, where they were severely opposed and suffered many losses. In November 1943, the remnants of the FTP-MOI in Paris, twenty-three members headed by Missak Manouchian, fell into the net of the French collaborationist forces. This was the end of the era of the FTP-MOI in Paris and the beginning of the "Trial of the 23" and a propaganda campaign against the "criminal army." The campaign was known for its infamous Red Poster, which was plastered all over Paris and presented the entire French Resistance as a bandit crew — all of them foreigners, most of them Jews.

But in the Vichy zone, the MOI-FTP groups remained fully active until the liberation of France. There, unlike in Paris, though the Jews were everywhere and sometimes even predominant, there were no specifically Jewish units. In Lyon, as in Grenoble and Toulouse, they fought side-by-side with Italians, Spaniards, Poles, anti-Nazi Germans and others. Veterans of the International Brigades occupied the leadership positions in many of these groups. Joseph's memoir is a rare eyewitness account of the life of a young resistance activist who was engaged in a Communist Jewish organization, while not a Communist himself, and who was then transferred to a fighting unit directly under the orders of the Party. This course of events allows him to describe a large range of resistance activities, to expose the sensitive relations between Jews and non-Jews in some Resistance groups, to describe the dangers the resisters were exposed to on an everyday basis and to portray the chaos of the last months of occupation, when French fascist groups and Resistance groups were fighting everywhere. His sharp eye does not leave anything in the dark.

Post-war

On August 25, 1944, Paris was liberated, and General de Gaulle marched along the Champs-Élysées and was greeted by an enthusiastic Parisian crowd. Another era had begun in France, although it took until May 8, 1945, for the German army to surrender.

For Jews all across Europe, the first priority was to reunite with the remaining members of their families, those who survived, and learn about their ordeals during the war years. For the different Jewish communities, the objective was to reorganize and reconstruct a Jewish social network. For the Zionist organizations, the development of the Yishuv in Palestine by massive emigration of the surviving Jews, against the will of the British government, would soon become the focus of their activities.

Joseph's trajectory in the post-war years is unique — the way each life is absolutely unique — yet it reflects the lives of many others and bears testimony, once again, to crucial historical events. His insight is particularly interesting as it succeeds in capturing the nuances of specific situations: the changed status of a Resistance fighter while travelling in liberated France — once an ostracized Jew and now a respected citizen; the determination of a Zionist to contribute to the creation of a sovereign state for Jews; the thread between illegality during the Resistance years and Zionist activism; military experience now used in service of a nation fighting for its existence; the peculiarities of kibbutz life during the formative years of the Yishuv and then the State of Israel; and finally, the way back to a "normal" life. Joseph ends his memoir with the death of his mother. This moving decision is highly significant — the death of his mother marked, as it does for many, a turning point in his life. From then on, the most important concrete link with his past was gone, and the past faded into the distance. The reason why this memoir is so special has much to do with the impressive trajectory of its author, but also with his remarkable sensitivity.

Renée Poznanski
Ben Gurion University of the Negev
2018

SOURCES

Cames, Pierre. *Cazaubon: chronique des années de guerre, 1939–1945.* Antony: P. Cames, 2002.

Farmer, Sarah. *Martyred Village: Commemorating the 1944 Massacre at Oradour-sur-Glane.* Berkeley: University of California Press, 2000.

Gildea, Robert. *Fighters in the Shadows: A New History of the French Resistance.* Cambridge, MA: Belknap Press of Harvard University Press, 2015.

Gourfinkel, Nina. *L'Autre Patrie.* Paris: Seuil, 1953.

Griffioen, Pim and Zeller, Ron. "La persécution des Juifs en Belgique et aux Pays-Bas pendant la Seconde Guerre mondiale: Une analyse comparative." *Cahiers d'Histoire du Temps Présent (CHTP-BEG)* 5 (1999): 73–132.

Grubel, Fred and Mecklenburg, Frank. "Leipzig: Profile of a Jewish Community during the first years of Nazi Germany." *The Leo Baeck Institute Year Book* 42, no. 1 (January 1997): 155–188.

Harmelin, Wilhelm. "Jews in the Leipzig Fur Industry." *The Leo Baeck Institute Year Book* 9, no. 1 (January 1964): 239–266.

Jackson, Julian. *France: The Dark Years, 1940–1944.* New York: Oxford University Press, 2003.

Kaplan, Marion. *Between Dignity and Despair: Jewish Life in Nazi Germany.* New York: Oxford University Press, 1999.

Marrus, Michael R. and Paxton, Robert O. "The Nazis and the Jews in Occupied Western Europe, 1940–1944." *The Journal of Modern History* 54, no. 4 (December 1982): 687–714.

Marrus, Michael R. and Paxton, Robert O. *Vichy France and the Jews.* Stanford: Stanford University Press, 1995.

Poznanski, Renée. *Jews in France during World War II.* Hanover, NH: Brandeis University Press / USHMM, University Press of New England, 2001.

Poznanski, Renée. "On Jews, Frenchmen, Communists, and the Second World War." *Studies in Contemporary Jewry* xx (2004): 168–198.

Poznanski, Renée. *Propagandes et Persécutions, la Résistance et le "Problème juif."* Paris: Fayard, 2008.

Schleunes, Karl. *The Twisted Road to Auschwitz: Nazi Policy towards German Jews.* Urbana: University of Illinois Press, 1990.

Schröter, Michael and Tögel, Christfried. "The Leipzig Episode in Freud's Life (1859): A New Narrative on the Basis of Recently Discovered Documents." *The Psychoanalytic Quarterly* 76, no. 1 (2007): 193–215.

Simonsen, Jon Gunnar Molstre. "Perfect Targets – Antisemitism and Eastern Jews in Leipzig, 1919–1923." *The Leo Baeck Institute Year Book* (2006).

Steinberg, Maxime. *Un pays occupé et ses Juifs, La Belgique, entre France et Pays-Bas.* Gerpinnes: Quorum, 1999.

Wieviorka, Olivier. *The French Resistance.* Cambridge, MA: Belknap Press of Harvard University Press, 2016.

Willingham II, Robert Allen. *Jews in Leipzig: Nationality and Community in the 20th Century.* Austin: University of Texas at Austin, 2005.

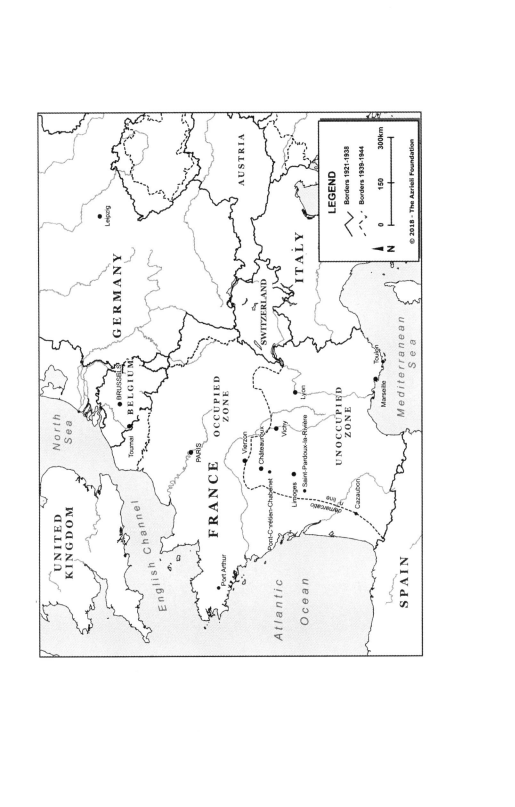

LEGEND

Borders 1921-1938
Borders 1939-1944

0   150   300km

© 2018 – The Azrieli Foundation

N

UNITED KINGDOM

North Sea

English Channel

Atlantic Ocean

GERMANY

Leipzig

BELGIUM

BRUSSELS

Tournai

PARIS

FRANCE

OCCUPIED ZONE

Port Arthur

Vierzon

Châteauroux

Pont-Chrétien-Chabenet

Limoges

Saint-Pardoux-la-Rivière

Vichy

Lyon

UNOCCUPIED ZONE

Cazaubon

demarcation line

SPAIN

AUSTRIA

SWITZERLAND

ITALY

Mediterranean Sea

Marseille

Toulon

With thanks to my daughter, Eve Schwarz, whose hard work and dedication in editing the first draft of my manuscript made the publication of this book possible.

This story is dedicated to the memory of my mother, Chava (Eva) Schwarzberg, the most courageous woman I have ever known. I also dedicate this to my mother's eight brothers and sisters and their children, almost all of whom perished in the concentration camps in Poland. Only one of her brothers, my uncle, survived, without his children.

To my adoptive father, Noach (Natan) Swieczka, who did his utmost to educate and teach me up to the age of fourteen. He was mobilized by the Polish army-in-exile in May 1940 in Paris and was later delivered by the French government of Philippe Pétain and Pierre Laval to Camp Vernet, where he was held as a foreigner who was considered suspect or dangerous to the public order. Later in life, I learned that he was deported to Auschwitz on August 19, 1942, from Drancy, the internment camp just north of Paris. No one from his immediate or extended family survived the war. I missed Noach dearly, especially in my teenage years, when my hope of reuniting with him was still very much alive.

This story is also dedicated to all my teachers, especially Daniel Kazman, my devoted classroom teacher in Leipzig, Germany, who was deported in 1942 from Leipzig to a concentration camp in Poland where he perished, along with most of the other teachers from the Carlebach School in Leipzig. My other teachers, Dr. Yosef Burg and Rabbi Carlebach, emigrated in the 1930s.

Lastly, I dedicate this to Victor Vermont, whose real name was Vila Glasberg. Vermont was arrested by the Gestapo at the Château du Bégué in Cazaubon, France, on August 16, 1943, and was held in several prisons in Paris before being deported to Auschwitz. L'Abbé (Father) Alexandre Glasberg, Vermont's older brother, survived the war after saving many hundreds of Jews and other people from the Nazis through his organization, Amitié Chrétienne (Christian Fellowship). Vermont and Father Glasberg were recognized by Yad Vashem as Righteous Among the Nations. Alexandre Glasberg was a true friend to Israel after the war, as he facilitated complicated operations that enabled Holocaust survivors to immigrate to British Mandate Palestine and, later, the State of Israel.

Part I

A Time of Hope and Fear

I was born in Leipzig, Germany, on June 17, 1926, and lived there with my stepfather, Noach, and my mother, Chava. I will start my story in 1932, since it seems to me that I have retained some reliable memories from this troublesome period. In 1932 Leipzig had a population of about 713,000, with a Jewish population of approximately 11,600. Leipzig was a typical old European city and a bustling commercial centre. It was also known for its raw furs and the manufacturing of fur coats, jackets and accessories. Our family resided in a non-Jewish district of Leipzig located at the southern border of the very busy commercial inner city, which was encircled by a busy road and street-car line. The Jewish district was directly opposite our neighbourhood on the outside of this ring road. I entered the public school system in 1932; since June was the cut-off for school registration, I was the youngest in my class throughout my school years. Living in the non-Jewish district of Leipzig meant that I went to a non-Jewish school, and as far as I am aware, I was the only Jewish child in this school.

Politically, 1932 was a very turbulent year in Germany. The Nazis were on the brink of power, and the streets were often extremely riotous. My classmates and I already knew the differences between the various police units. We often witnessed violence in the streets and tried to make some sense of it all. The disquiet and anxiety of the adults around us affected us, and we listened intently to their discussions and arguments. Hitler's antisemitic rhetoric was extremely disturbing and worrisome to every Jew. But people do not stop living and hoping, and there seemed to be an abundance of opinions as to why the Nazis would not make it to power.

However, the Nazis did make it to power in 1933. I remember vividly the elections and the *Ja* (Yes) vote for the Nazis. Nearly everyone on the street sported a glittering silver or brass swastika pin marked with a *Ja* on their jackets or garments. Since I was one of the very few who was not wearing the *Ja* pin of national unity and purpose, I stood out. I felt like a stranger in the country in which I was born. The national rhetoric was intense and forceful, and for a child to be different and not part of this rhetoric was traumatic. The sweeping marches and songs, all intended to rally the people to the Nazis, had a very strange effect on me: on the one hand, there was wonder at the power and enthusiasm being demonstrated; on the other, I questioned what would happen to us, the Jews, and to me. It was challenging for me as a child to understand what lay in store for us as Jews.

In the spring of 1933, shortly after the election, as I was on my way home from school, I noticed pairs of uniformed Nazi SA men standing in front of several stores that were branded with the word *Jude*, Jew, written in big letters. In some cases, these stores were also marked with a prominent Star of David beside the *Jude*. I stood there in front of the stores with other onlookers, wondering and worrying.

My sister, Lea, was born in March 1933, and my parents sent me to stay with a Christian family for a week. They were friends and clients of my parents, and I did not experience any discrimination from this couple.

My family and I lived in an apartment at the back of a four-storey building, where my parents also did their sewing work during the day. To reach our apartment and workshop, we had to cross a yard and a porch, which were dotted with laundry. At the front of the building there was a sign indicating that there was a tailor shop inside. One day, just in front of the entrance to our building, there stood two Nazi SA men questioning every individual who entered: "Where to?" One lady's response was "to Schwarzberg." However, this response did not raise the suspicions of the SA men, as Schwarzberg was not recognized as a Jewish name.

On another occasion, just after my school's religion class was dismissed, I was assaulted by a group of children who blamed me for the death of Jesus and said that I deserved punishment. It was distressful and incomprehensible to me, and I had no idea what they were talking about. I never did complain or even tell my parents about the incident; I must have felt the futility of doing so.

I also recall the dismissal of the Jewish state employees, including Jewish professors at state universities all over Germany. On April 7, 1933, the Law for the Restoration of the Professional Civil Service was implemented. The first major law to impede the rights of Jews in Germany, it required that Jewish and "politically unreliable" civil servants and employees, such as communists, be excluded from state service. This event was the topic of numerous discussions at home, as my parents had friends and acquaintances who were affected by this dismissal.

In the streets no extreme changes were noticeable, except for the threatening and unrelenting antisemitic rhetoric repeatedly proclaimed over the radio and in the newspapers. My parents still had their predominantly Christian clientele, but slowly this changed. I was responsible for doing the rounds every Sunday to collect payment from clients. There was a sense of unease in some of the families I visited, or the family was split between those opposed to and those for the Nazi Party. It was not uncommon to hear loud and forceful differences of opinions in the same family. Now, upon my arrival in these homes, the air was tense, whereas previously there had been a welcome reception and a smiling face accompanied by laughter, familiarity, cake and chocolate drinks.

Opposite our apartment there was a narrow street bordered by three- to four-storey houses with inner courtyards containing

,

additional housing units or workshops. Down this narrow street there was a building with a large window where I could view a very big, prominently displayed map of Spain that showed the developments in the Spanish Civil War. There were pins representing Franco, the leader of the Nationalists, and his supporters, and others representing the Republicans and the International Brigades. It was almost a ritual for me to stand at the window, observing people and listening to their dialogue. I was saddened whenever the Republicans suffered a setback. This was my earliest education in politics and military strategy.

Nazi propaganda was abundant and spread with great vigour. One day I stood at another window where an enormous picture of Hitler was displayed. Probably not conscious of what I was doing, I swung a stick that I was holding, as if to beat Hitler. Suddenly I was interrupted by an SS officer standing behind me, asking me what I was doing. Overwhelmed with fear, I ran away as fast as I could, weaving in different directions through the streets for as long as possible. Luckily there were no consequences, and I never dared tell my parents of my brief error in judgment.

During several of my summer vacations, my mother took me to Poland, where we visited close relatives in Warsaw, Lodz and Magnuszew, a little village near the Vistula River. For me, Poland was a unique experience compared to what I was accustomed to in Germany. People lived and worked in very cramped quarters, and the homes lacked the modern conveniences that we had in Leipzig. In Germany the apartments and the toilets had running water, and the toilets were within the same unit as the apartments; in older buildings, the toilet was on the same floor, just outside of the apartment or between the apartment floors on the landings. In Warsaw there were large apartment blocks, and the toilets, which didn't have running water, were in the inner courtyards. I sometimes had to run down five flights to reach the toilet. There were also fewer paved streets in the Polish cities, and more horse-drawn carriages and wagons than cars and trucks.

My vacations in Poland often lasted six weeks, allowing me to experience and get accustomed to the vast difference in lifestyle compared to Leipzig. There was food in Poland that was not as abundantly available in Germany in quantity or quality: goose liver, fat Polish sausages, apple strudel, fruits, bakery products and dairy products, such as cheeses and butter. The food was heavenly.

I also enjoyed the slower pace of life in Magnuszew, as well as the people. I liked bathing in the Vistula River, where we found a little white sandy island with some vegetation on it and enjoyed watching the ships go by. We would stay at a farmer's house and join my grandfather and grandmother for our meals. Our delicious breakfasts usually consisted of garden cucumbers and tomatoes, fresh bread and butter made from homemade yogourt. The cream of the yogourt was skimmed and placed into a bottle that was shaken vigorously until butter emerged. Ducklings, goslings and chicks ran freely in the kitchen of the farmer's home. They were kept there in order to protect them until they were strong enough to live in the yard and fend for themselves. It was a real pleasure for us children to catch these soft creatures and hold them in our hands. There were also many flocks of geese from all of the neighbouring farms that were quite aggressive, and I learned to keep my distance from them.

My grandfather would purchase the fruit harvests from the farmers in the early spring when the trees were in bloom. While living on the farm in a tent-like structure, he would watch over and tend to the orchard; then, when the fruits were ripe, he would collect them and transport the harvest (a day-long venture) to the Warsaw market by horse-drawn wagon. One of his married sons had a big stand at the Warsaw market. On one occasion I witnessed my grandfather being attacked by young boys who were trying to steal fruit from the wagon. He used his whip, striking forcefully in all directions to hold the attackers at bay and to accelerate the horses to a running pace. I also witnessed Jewish boys who were playing in the street verbally and then physically attack a gentile Polish boy. For me this was a boldness I hadn't seen before and perhaps a way for the Jewish children to release their frustrations at the antisemitism that they were enduring. The one thing that Poland did not lack was an abundance of antisemitism.

Growing Up Fast

In 1935 the Nuremberg Laws were enacted, barring marriage between German Jews and gentile Germans and removing citizenship rights from those who supposedly did not have "German blood." A law against overcrowding in schools and universities was passed in April 1933, gradually restricting the attendance of Jewish children in public schools; in Leipzig Jewish students were expelled from schools in September 1935. I was then transferred to a Jewish school in the Carlebach School building in the Jewish quarter, on the northern perimeter of the inner city, quite a distance by foot, as I lived on the southern perimeter of the inner city. I had two friends who lived not too far from me, and we would walk to and from school together. Walking through the very busy inner city, we always managed to discover something interesting. Our parents were often worried about us, as some of our wanderings took us three to five hours rather than the forty-five minutes the walk should have taken.

In 1936 we moved to Leipzig's Jewish district. My parents' Christian clientele had dwindled to just a few customers, and it was necessary for them to find other clients in the Jewish neighbourhood. My parents rented a six-room apartment, which we divided as follows: my parents' bedroom, one or two rooms used for their work, a large living room with four picture windows and my small room. The remaining one or two bedrooms were rented to subtenants, some of whom were very interesting people.

One of our tenants was a gentleman in his thirties. He was a musician and a socialist youth leader, a very principled person. He was often visited by his friends, and the Gestapo came to our apartment looking for him on several occasions, which endeared him to my family even more. Unfortunately, he eventually left our apartment and we did not hear from him again. During the time that he was with us, I would go to his mother's home in the countryside for a few days or a week during the school holidays. One incident that occurred while I was there stands out in my memory. I used to visit a nearby farmer who had two sons, one of whom was my age or slightly older, and I often helped with the chores on the farm so that the boy and I could play afterward. On one occasion, the farmer's son suddenly started hurling hurtful antisemitic insults at me. His father was surprised to come upon this scene and acted immediately and forcefully, giving his son a strong beating. I never returned to the farm after this incident.

Our other subtenant was a single Jewish woman with a very broad education. Her main treasure was her extensive, diverse library of books. I had free access to her library, which was mostly beyond my level of comprehension. In any case, I kept reading the books, even if I didn't understand all that I read.

My mother managed her shop, making dresses, suits and coats. Sometimes she would work on her own and sometimes she hired help. The ready-made garment industry was not as developed then as it is today, so people still required made-to-measure garments. My father sold lingerie and stockings to private customers and to stores. It was a difficult way to make a living. Both of my parents spoke German without a Polish or Yiddish accent. My father also spoke high school level English and French, as well as fluent Polish and Russian. He was able to communicate with people from the Balkan states when they visited Leipzig twice a year for the famous commercial fairs. But Hebrew was his favourite language, and he invested much time and effort to improve his knowledge of it. Each Saturday I had to sit with him to receive lessons in Hebrew, in addition to my twice-weekly lessons in the Talmud Torah. When I arrived in Israel after the war, those long-forgotten lessons were revived and were an enormous help to me in overcoming the language hurdles more rapidly than any of my friends who arrived in Israel with me.

Our new apartment was very close to my school. In school, our class teacher, Daniel Kazman, taught sports, music and German. He was also a sports writer. He was a forceful disciplinarian; his way was the only possible way, and he was not afraid to use physical punishment. Discipline was absolute in his classroom, and in his presence no one dared to be the least controversial. He knew how to instill knowledge and important character traits, such as accuracy, reliability and taking responsibility.

There were also other interesting teachers, such as our religion teacher, who often took time to explain his version of political events, adding his own commentaries, especially on the Italian war in Ethiopia — the Second Italo-Ethiopian War, a colonial war fought from October 1935 to 1939. Our geography teacher also imparted his knowledge and opinions about the conflicts and tensions experienced worldwide.

There was a general uneasiness in hearing all of the antisemitic rhetoric around us, and even as children we were concerned for our lives and safety. We grew up fast during that time, but we also remained children, playing in parks and fields and going on trips to the forests on weekends with parents or youth organizations. My family's apartment was located at the entrance to a very large park, and we often went on little excursions to play ball or to wander alone or in groups. In the winter the park was the place for skating, sleigh riding and downhill or cross-country skiing. However, even during our moments of leisure and relaxation, we had to confront the practical results of the antisemitic education of the German population. We were verbally and sometimes physically attacked. Over time these attacks became more frequent and forceful.

I recall the 1936 trans-Atlantic flight from Germany to the United States by the Hindenburg Zeppelin. Extremely propagandized by the German media, this event was hailed as a super-achievement of the German people and used as proof of their superiority. The propaganda circulated for weeks without interruption. Posters of the event embellished every possible window and place. It elicited strange feelings in me. On the one hand I wanted to identify with such triumphs and would have liked to feel that I could participate in the national pride; on the other hand, there was a clear understanding that we Jews were no longer included in German society.

By the end of 1937, we again moved within the Jewish district, to a place not far from our previous home but in a much nicer neighbourhood with more impressive buildings and near another entrance to the same park. Our building was five storeys high and had about ten apartments in it. The base of the building up to the first half-floor was built with granite blocks. We had a corner apartment that was very roomy, with a large kitchen and a big balcony that was accessible from my parents' room. My parents grew tomatoes on the balcony. The window in my room faced the street, and in front of my window was a gas-operated street lamp. I could sometimes see a man lighting or extinguishing this lamp with a long stick. The lamp served me well when I wanted to read after my parents imposed lights out.

This apartment had the added bonus that our neighbours just across the hallway, Mr. and Mrs. Hesse, were my parents' close friends. I liked this couple very much and called them Aunt and Uncle Hesse. They were a childless couple somewhat older than my parents, and they treated me like their son, welcoming me into their home. The atmosphere in their home was so different from ours. The rooms were decorated with inherited antique furniture, antique lamps and Persian carpets. Mr. Hesse was tall, broad-shouldered and very athletic. He worked as an office supply salesman, and his office was filled with a Gestetner copier, typewriters and other interesting machinery that I was permitted to use. The Hesse family were good friends and were later there with us to share some very troubling times. They both had German-Jewish ancestry going back many generations, and they considered themselves to be Germans of the Jewish faith. They were very proud of being what they thought of as "real" Germans. Mr. Hesse was very impressive — he had been an artillery officer in the German army in World War I, and was wounded and awarded the Iron Cross medal. He had a limp when he walked as a result of this war wound.

The economic life of Jews in Germany was constantly deteriorating. New government edicts, rules and regulations were aimed at extinguishing any possibility for Jews to earn a living. Many good friends of my parents left the country to immigrate to Palestine, Argentina, Brazil, France and Great Britain. As anxieties grew, so did discussions of what to do next and where to go to escape the increasing restrictions we faced. For a while my father tried to apply for an immigration certificate to Palestine. He enlisted in *hachsharah*, a training program for new immigrants, but he found it extremely difficult and physically demanding work, and it required him to forfeit his remunerative position and regular income for the time that he spent learning. In any case, his efforts were to no avail, as he was considered too old to obtain the immigration certificate.

At school we faced constant changes in staff and students. There was an amalgamation of the seventh and eighth grades, and we counted forty students in our class, rather than the typical thirty. New teachers were brought in to teach at the school. They were mostly not educated as teachers, but were vastly overqualified people who were banned from their professions and had no other employment options. They were mostly industrialists and academics, such as Dr. Yosef Burg, who later held various ministerial positions in the Israeli government. Our teachers emphasized and encouraged immigration to any country that would accept us. They also tried to prepare us mentally for some of the drastic changes that were coming. Most of the Jewish youth met at the different Zionist organizations, which offered diverse activities like sports, lectures and other social activities aimed to prepare us for immigration to Palestine. It was made clear to us that emigration was necessary for our survival.

The Tomarkins, friends of my parents, had to give up their grocery store, but they continued to sell groceries from their home. They had a large family with six children, all of them older than I was. One child after the other left for Palestine. When a child left, it was always very tense for the parents and the other siblings. A wealth of books was left behind by those children, and I had free access to them when I desired. I also received a bicycle that had belonged to one of the children. I sometimes assisted with their grocery deliveries and received modest compensation.

Sometime around 1937, the secretary of the Jewish community, one of my parents' customers, noticed that I helped my parents in many ways, especially by collecting payment from their clients. She asked my parents to allow me to collect money for the Jewish community on Sundays. The secretary prepared a list of people for me to visit, and I went out almost every Sunday morning to a different district of the city with my receipt book in hand, doing the job that adults had done before me. I must have been about eleven years old at that time. It was a tremendous experience, exposing me to the most expensive and beautiful Jewish homes in the city. Generally speaking, it was a well-off community with quite a number of wealthy people, especially those who worked in the international fur industry. I visited some splendid homes in which there was lovely, valuable furniture and original artworks. Most of the people were very nice and received me well — sometimes extremely warmly — providing me with cake and chocolate because of my young age. People also gave generously, which I believe was the secretary's primary motivation in choosing me for this job. The amounts collected were in the hundreds of marks, as people had a definite impression that the community must band together and that the more fortunate had an obligation to help those who had no or few resources.

The year 1938 was a traumatic watershed for Jewish life in Germany, and for me and my family it was an extremely distressing and dramatic time. Up until October 1938, the struggle for survival was becoming more difficult, yet the Jewish community somehow went on with its daily existence. We tried to eke out a living and talked about emigration. I remember reading about those who succeeded in emigrating illegally and smuggling out their assets, and about those who were caught at the border. Life was filled with tension, yet there was still a degree of routine.

The summer holidays must have been uneventful for me as I have no recollection of them. At the end of September, my mother and sister, Lea, visited my mother's family in Poland, but I was left behind with my father. I suspect this was either because of the school schedule or perhaps because of a lack of financial means. By the end of October 1938, about 17,000 Polish and stateless Jews had been gathered and sent to the German-Polish border. Poland did not willingly accept these Jews, and many of them were left without adequate shelter or food for the cold winter months. These refugees became a source of great friction between Germany and Poland. As a result of this instability, my father sent a telegram to my mother requesting that she delay her return from Poland.

The entire Jewish community was in upheaval but rallied together to support those in need. The Polish consulate official in Leipzig had good relations with the Polish-Jewish community. He offered shelter to the Polish Jews who arrived at the consulate or at his residence. There were limited resources at the consulate to shelter such large numbers, and the overcrowding stretched its capacity for shelter, sanitation and food supplies. The Jews from the community who held passports or had more privileged standing dared to move freely and provided much-needed support, food and other necessities to those who were confined to the consulate. The community came together in a splendid demonstration of mutual assistance. Several months later, in January 1939, the Polish and German authorities would agree that the deportations would stop, and the deportees were allowed to emigrate or return to Germany temporarily.

～

On the night of November 9, 1938, I woke up to the sound of moving furniture. The Hesses, our neighbours from across the landing, were in our apartment with my father. Everyone was extremely agitated. People were moving to and fro, pushing furniture across the floor to blockade the door and crossing the room to peek out the window through closed shutters. Frantic phone calls were being made to the police, who only said that they were aware of the situation — a rash of violence being perpetrated against Jews — and that they would be on their way shortly. The police did arrive eventually, very late at night, after the Nazis had completed their destruction.

As I peeked out from the shutters, using extreme care not to be noticed, I witnessed one of my classmates, along with his younger brother and his parents, being severely beaten as all of their belongings were thrown out into the street. About ten young men in brown uniforms screamed insults and struck them mercilessly with batons. My classmate's younger brother was tied by his neck to a bicycle and had to run after it for fear of being choked. He finally collapsed on the street, completely bruised and exhausted. Years later, in Israel in the late 1940s, I met this classmate and his brother, who had become a police sergeant.

My father and I received temporary salvation from a Danish woman and her twenty-year-old daughter. This woman was a loyal customer of my parents, and I had been invited several times to visit her impressive villa in the suburbs of Leipzig. She and her husband were very anti-Nazi. After the events of November 9–10, which became known as Kristallnacht, she came to my family and insisted that we accept her offer for a temporary safe haven in her home until the crisis had passed. My father asked to bring our neighbours, Mr. and Mrs. Hesse, and she agreed without hesitation. However, when my father brought this most generous offer to Mr. and Mrs. Hesse, Uncle Hesse vehemently declined. Although he was shaken from the recent events, Uncle Hesse still believed in his beloved Germany and clung to the illogical belief that this was just an isolated incident of a Nazi disturbance and that the fundamental character of the decent German would prevail. He had the notion that as a decorated German officer from World War I, he could not permit a band of unruly lawbreakers to chase him into hiding.

After a stealthy departure from our home and our safe arrival at the Danish woman's villa, my father sent a coded telegram to my mother to let her know that "Mr. Chorban" — from the Yiddish word *khurbn*, meaning destruction — had come to visit us. We remained at the villa for about a week, closely monitoring the Nazi propaganda. Our host would not take any compensation from us nor did she wish for us to go. However, my father understood that hiding at her villa was not a long-term solution. When we returned to our home, we learned that Uncle Hesse had been taken away by a group of SS men, and his protestations were of no assistance to him. We later found out that Uncle Hesse was taken to Sachsenhausen, one of the first Nazi concentration camps.

My father then went into hiding; I don't know where. The Nazis were gathering Jews without nationalities, and my father's official status, even though he was born in Poland, was of no nationality; he held what was called a Nansen passport, which was issued by the League of Nations to stateless refugees. I was left in the care of the Tomarkin family. My mother returned from Poland, but since she was unsure of the situation in Germany, she had left Lea in Poland in the care of her sister. The first item on my mother's agenda was to smuggle my father into Belgium. There was abundant proof to confirm the rumours that the Jews who lacked a nationality were being seized by the Nazis and deported to concentration camps. One day my parents simply said goodbye to me and left me with the Tomarkin family. About a week later, my mother returned home to Leipzig. In retrospect, I never had the feeling of being abandoned. Rather there was a pervasive sense of needing to struggle for survival. There was an understanding within the Jewish community of a pact to defend and survive that pervaded our daily life. A short time after my mother returned from the Belgian border, the police arrived at our home to arrest my father. They came back many times as they did not believe my mother when she told them that she did not know where he was.

The rule for German-Jewish nationals was that if you could show a visa and proof of paid transportation, the Nazis would let you leave. Shanghai was the only place in the world at that time that did not require a visa for entry. After six weeks in Sachsenhausen, and after Mrs. Hesse persisted in showing her husband's military decorations to anyone who would pay attention and displaying her coveted tickets to Shanghai, Mr. Hesse was permitted to return home. We were all shocked at his condition. This tall, strong, muscular, athletic, proud German officer was a broken man, his spirit completely destroyed. We now saw a shrunken being who cried without reprieve. Uncle Hesse sat on his bed and had great difficulty moving. He had physical and emotional wounds and experienced constant pain all over. His brother had also been imprisoned at Sachsenhausen and returned home in the same condition.

I listened with rapt attention to the stories that Uncle Hesse told me of his experiences in Sachsenhausen. They gave me a clear vision of what the Germans could do to me and showed me that I must resolve to escape if caught. Uncle Hesse also made me realize that I would have to struggle very hard for survival. Unbeknownst to him, Uncle Hesse can be credited with providing me with knowledge of the immense threat posed by the Germans, which was invaluable to me and contributed greatly to my survival.

After Kristallnacht, whenever I met my school friends, the topic of conversation concentrated on the events that we had just experienced. There were many stories about people's heroic behaviour. One that I remember was of the kosher butcher and his sons putting up a courageous fight after the Nazis invaded their home; other stories involved German anti-Nazis, as well as brave, fierce dogs defending their victimized owners. It became apparent that there was the occasional vain resistance against the Nazis. One especially significant and tragic story was that of Dr. Cohen, an ear, nose and throat specialist, who had removed my tonsils. His office was always full of patients, despite the anti-Jewish propaganda discrediting Jewish doctors. One morning a group of Nazis invaded his office, ignoring the waiting patients, and mercilessly beat the doctor to death.

Other events that have remained in my memory are the destruction of two large synagogues by fire and the ruin of various other places of Jewish worship and of many landmark Jewish businesses in Leipzig. After Kristallnacht, Jewish businesses that hadn't been physically destroyed were "Aryanized" — most significantly, Leipzig's fur industry. The fur industry had been introduced into Leipzig by Jewish merchants from Poland and Russia during the Middle Ages. In the eighteenth and especially nineteenth centuries, these merchants were protected by the Saxon kings because of the wealth and prosperity that they brought. In just one night, Kristallnacht destroyed this established and renowned industry. This was a sad blow to Leipzig's Jewish community as it was the last bastion of income and wealth for the Jews of that city. For my friends and for me, it was a profound loss, as we had enjoyed wandering through the vibrant fur district. There was constant activity there: trucks loading and unloading, freight elevators running slowly up and down, men throwing pelts and bundles of fur to each other — the air filled with the smell of fur and leather. My friends and I would often ride the freight elevators until we were chased away.

Life continued with even more difficulty. In school there was constant change and disruption. Many of my schoolmates and friends were no longer there. There was no formal curriculum, or any curriculum, that was strictly adhered to. Everyone was focused on the political circumstances, or rather the politics of survival. The only opportunity for any relief was with our class teacher, Daniel Kazman, who took us out as often as possible to play sports and compete in light athletics, which kept us fit and in good spirits. He even went so far as to give up his afternoons to organize games that were open to any of his students who wanted to participate. There were always many enthusiastic participants.

We children, and perhaps the Jewish community as a whole, experienced feelings of apprehension yet hoped that somehow we would overcome this adversity. There were Zionist films showing the pioneers in British Mandate Palestine developing and clearing the wilderness manually and with heavy equipment. They were pictured hard at work building a drainage system in the Hula Valley in the northern Galilee. Of course these Zionists looked very happy performing this back-breaking work. I realize only now how important this positive portrayal of Zionist ideology was for us. While Nazi propaganda was portraying Jews as unfit, useless workers, we had an antidote that proved to us that the Nazi party line was a lie.

Escape to Brussels

Now that my father had left for Belgium, any idea we had of immigrating to Poland was no longer possible. So my mother wrote to her sister in Poland, where my sister, Lea, had been left, in order to make arrangements to bring Lea back home to Germany. My mother's sister did not provide my mother with any information as to how and when Lea would be returned; instead, she answered my mother's questions by saying that Lea had fallen slightly ill and could not travel at present. More than a month passed before my mother wrote with more forceful insistence to have Lea returned. The response was that Lea was ill with diphtheria and was hospitalized for about two months. Lea became extremely weak and emaciated as a result. She was released from the hospital in March 1939. After her release, my mother arranged to have her sister bring Lea to Guben, a city on the Polish-German border, where my mother was to meet them. As it turned out, this was not such an easy feat to accomplish. When she arrived at the border crossing, my mother was confronted with various bureaucratic procedures meant to make it difficult to cross the border. However, my mother was bold and persistent and convinced the Germans to allow her to meet her sister and Lea at the halfway point, from where she was able to bring Lea across the border to Germany.

Now six years old, Lea was extremely weak and unable to walk even the shortest distance. In addition to her baggage, my mother had to carry Lea all the way to the train station and then home. My mother returned to Leipzig completely exhausted. During her absence I was cared for by our friends the Tomarkins, where I willingly stayed. My mother now had the full-time occupation of nursing Lea back to health. Her intention had been to meet my father in Belgium, but Lea's illness, as well as my father's escape, took a toll on our finances. As a result, my mother sold some of our household possessions, such as furniture and leftover merchandise, and she was grateful for whatever funds she was offered, mostly by loyal customers.

In May 1939 my mother arranged for a transport company to pack and send my father a lift, a large crate containing my parents' bedroom furniture, my mother's sewing machine, bedding, blankets and all of our garments, including new shoes and other items that could be sold in order to cover possible emergencies. As soon as all of our belongings were out of the apartment, we went to stay temporarily with friends. My mother calculated that she would not have sufficient funds to cover all of the expenses required to escape Germany with a group of smugglers. We needed money for the smugglers' fees, railway fares from Leipzig to Cologne and lodging expenses in Cologne.

I was only thirteen, but I understood that the funds were necessary for our survival. Without saying anything to my mother, I visited some of the people from whom I used to collect money when I was helping the Jewish community. I explained our situation to them — that my father was already in Belgium, that we wished to be reunited with him and that my mother did not have enough money to pay the smugglers. I was able to garner sympathy and significant funds from nearly all the families I visited. Some of them asked that my mother pick up the money with me. My mother, astonished that I had set out on such a quest, came with me to collect the funds from those who requested her presence. Everyone we visited wished us the best and expressed their greatest hope for our success.

We then left Leipzig for Cologne. When we arrived we were lodged in a room in an apartment that was overcrowded with others who were waiting to flee Germany. Every day that we were there, new people arrived as others left. We stayed in Cologne for several days, each day costing us dearly in lodging fees, which fueled our desire to leave as soon as possible. But unfortunately we were not in control of when we left. During the day I strolled along the Rhine River and through the city. I had a good sense of direction and never had to ask how to get back to our home base. In any event, I instinctively knew that asking for directions would not be wise given our circumstances.

I remember that my mother paid one thousand marks to the smugglers for Lea and me to be smuggled over the Belgian border. She did not have enough money left to pay for a smuggler for herself. When the day finally came to leave Cologne, we were told in the morning that it would be our turn to leave that same afternoon. In the late afternoon, two cars came to our building to pick up those lucky enough to be selected to leave that day. I recall one of the cars distinctly; it was an Opel Kadett, and there was a young woman in the front seat beside the driver. The second car had only a driver. Since the cars were medium to small in size, and we were a total of six adults and two children, not including the smugglers, they were quite crowded. My sister sat on the lap of a stranger. Yet the feeling was that we were all united through our perilous endeavour to escape Nazi Germany. We all felt the tension and knew that we had to follow the smugglers' directions.

As we started our journey, the young woman in the front seat of our car explained what was going to happen next, provided that all went according to plan. She gave us detailed instructions: It would be dark as we approached the border, about an hour away; on the right side of the road we would see a big truck stopped; the hood would be up and the driver would be bent over the engine pretending to do repairs. Our cars would each stop behind the truck, but not at the same time. We were to run from the car and climb into the truck and hide behind the boxes and barrels; Lea and I were to climb into the driver's cabin. All of us were sternly warned not to run into the highway lanes and to avoid any possible light source. Our car was the second one to reach the truck, and we started moving shortly after we boarded it. I am not sure how long we rode in the truck, but I remember that every time a vehicle approached, we had to duck as low as possible in the cabin to avoid being caught in the glow of its headlights.

We successfully finished the first leg of our journey and were now ready for the next stage. The driver explained to us that he would be stopping on the right side of the road and that we were to run as fast as we possibly could to the left behind his vehicle, away from the lights, across the road and into a field where someone would be waiting to meet us. When the truck stopped we all jumped out. I grabbed Lea's hand and ran into the night, into an unknown field in the middle of nowhere. After what seemed like an eternity of running in the darkness, we saw a man crouched in the field. He whispered, "Go faster and further, straight ahead." It was a tremendous relief to hear a voice giving us direction. We passed two more such guiding angels. Running in the dark fields was not an easy task. I tripped into holes, dragging my sister by the hand behind me. Lea did not complain, cry or speak. She conformed to the circumstances, as did everyone, with extreme silence.

After running for what seemed like forever, we were told that we could sit or lie down on the ground to relax and gather our energy. There were now four smugglers in our midst, all farmers in the region who, if found, could justify being there in a field by themselves. They told us about the next stage of our journey through the fields. One of the smugglers was to stay with us. The others were to fan out around us at about a fifty- to seventy-metre distance. If any one of them encountered a potentially perilous situation they would light a pipe, in which case we were to fall to the ground in order to avoid discovery.

It was getting difficult for my sister to walk, so I started to carry her on my shoulders, no easy task for me as I was only thirteen years old. It was actually my birthday and bar mitzvah day — June 17, 1939. The leader from our group of smugglers noticed my struggles, and not wanting to be delayed, he started carrying Lea on his shoulders. From then on every man in the group silently agreed to take a turn carrying my sister on his back. We became a homogeneous group with one common goal: to make it to our next destination. We walked through fields, passed over and through fences, sank our feet into cow dung and other undesirable matter and rested for only short periods, until we arrived at the edge of a deep ravine. There we stopped and were told to lie on the ground, the leader with us. The other smugglers, as before, took up positions at a distance on each side of us and across the ravine. We waited quietly for awhile. Suddenly, we observed two Belgian police officers riding their bicycles along a path in the ravine. When it was certain that they had passed, we ducked low and swiftly ran across the path and across the ravine. We understood that we were in Belgian territory but still subject to being deported back to Germany; the Belgians did not want to encourage refugees to come into their country.

After our hasty departure from the truck, it took us approximately three hours of exhausting scurrying through the dark field to finally reach our destination — a farmhouse. The smugglers invited us in and gave us drinks and food and a place to rest. We stayed there for about an hour and then continued our trek for about an hour, until we reached the edge of a forest close to the highway. The next step of our journey was explained to us here. Two taxis were to collect us and deliver us to our respective destinations in Brussels. We were told that there was the possibility of roadblocks, which the drivers would attempt to break through. If there was any shooting, we were to lie down on the floors of the taxis, and they would try to escape at high speed. This possible version of events made us all very concerned, but of course we accepted what we were told without argument.

The two taxis arrived within a ten-minute interval of each other. Lea and I got in the second taxi and bid a hurried goodbye to the smugglers. We drove off into the dawn, driving quickly and steadily. I viewed the Belgian landscape with curiosity and remember passing a truck filled with Belgian police. When we arrived in Brussels, it was still morning. The taxi driver hired additional taxis from the railway station, which I discovered later was the Gare du Nord or Northern Station. The members of our group were then sent to their assigned destinations, and Lea and I were taken to our designated address on Rue Vanderhaegen in Brussels.

There I was met with the harsh reality that our accommodations were not going to be as pleasant as I'd anticipated. Lea and I walked up to the third floor of a very old building, where the people in a tailor shop had agreed to take us as tenants. It was a very crowded space that served as both living quarters and a workplace. The apartment was owned by the butcher, who had his shop at street level. He and his family lived on the floor above the shop. The tenants with whom we shared our apartment had one son who was about two years younger than I was. Unfortunately, their family life was not harmonious, and we had to endure constant yelling and screaming between the husband and wife. We didn't speak a common language and could barely communicate.

Rue Vanderhaegen was in the midst of a Jewish slum filled with hard-working Jews; it was not much different than what I'd experienced during my visits to my mother's family in Poland. There was a bakery, grocery, barber, shoemaker, tailor, milk store, butter and eggs store — all sorts of very small family-run stores at the front of very old houses. Each house had three or four storeys, where people lived in very small apartments. With time I learned that there were many other illegal immigrants in this neighbourhood, and not just Jewish ones. At the butcher's there was a German worker who had been fighting with the International Brigades in Spain. He was most likely a communist and would be arrested by the Germans if caught.

Many Jewish organizations around the world raised money to support Jewish refugees in Belgium so that the Belgian government would not send them back to Germany. These Jews did not have work permits, but since the funds provided by the Jewish organizations were inadequate to cover the most basic existence, many Jews had to work illegally.

The neighbourhood had its own economy based on the resources that were available; it provided work and supported the needs of the people living there. The tailor shops purchased old suits, had them cleaned and mended them or tailored them to fit new customers — mostly farmers, miners and other out-of-town dwellers. The tailors sold their goods at the marketplace on Saturdays and Sundays.

When Lea and I arrived at the apartment, my father was not there. He was being held in a camp for illegal immigrants but was soon permitted to come stay with us. My mother arrived at our new accommodations about one week after us and told us how she had managed to flee over the German-Belgian border. She had travelled by train to Eupen-Malmedy, near the border, and then started walking, crossing fields and forests, following the detailed directions given to her in Cologne. In the darkness of the night, not knowing exactly where she was, she entered the garage of a home in a Belgian village near the border. The owner of the home, a Belgian who was fluent in German, discovered her. Listening to her story, he told her to remain in his garage and closed the door. He later returned with some soup, as well as some old coats for her to cover herself with for the night. He told her that he would open the garage door for her before daybreak and leave it open when he drove away. He also explained in detail what direction she should go in and how far she should walk before taking the risk of boarding a train. She followed his directions and continued to walk for another day in order to distance herself from the German border. Only when she was at a safe distance did she board the train for Brussels. It was certainly a story of tremendous luck and courage. We were now all reunited, but my father had to return to the camp. My parents did not want to antagonize the authorities, as they could still deport us.

The circumstances we were in caused raw nerves and much conflict. The atmosphere on the street was heavy with the feeling that war would break out any day, and the consensus was that people wanted war, as they erroneously believed that the Allied forces would conquer Germany within six months.

The authorities soon allowed my father to leave the camp and live with us, and so we moved to more suitable accommodations. Our living space was still crowded but somewhat more organized than where we'd lived before. The lift that my mother had sent from Germany arrived, with my parents' bedroom furniture, clothing, linens, comforters and my mother's sewing machine. My mother immediately started sewing in order to make some money to purchase daily necessities. My father also started to make some money by giving Hebrew lessons. As refugees we were generally very poorly compensated. But whatever my parents earned helped supply us with decent meals.

My sister and I started school again in September 1939. I was placed in eighth grade without any knowledge of French or Flemish. When I reminded the teacher that I did not know or understand what he was teaching in math, he drily responded that math was the same in any language. It was evident to me that this teacher resented having to teach refugees. One teacher was sympathetic to me and two other refugees in the class. He would take us to the schoolyard during his own time and teach us French, pacing back and forth while repeating words in French and telling us their meanings. Our informal French classes lasted as long as we were in school.

When the war broke out between Germany and Poland in September 1939, developments did not match the hopes and expectations of the people in our community. With the help of the Soviets, who had signed the Molotov-Ribbentrop Pact with the Germans to divide Poland between them, Poland was defeated in a very short span of time. The optimists among us saw this as a temporary setback, predicting that once war started in the west, everything would be reversed and the Germans would be defeated in short order. Of course this was not the case.

People went about their daily lives, and we moved to larger accommodations with two rooms in a small building owned by a non-Jew and occupied mostly by Belgian Jews along with a few refugees from Germany. One of the rooms was long and deep, with a big window, and served as the bedroom for all of us. The other room, which had two large windows and access to the hallway, had multiple uses: kitchen, living room and my mother's workroom. There was a big stove that was used for cooking and baking, as well as to heat the rooms in the winter. We fed it with coal carefully, so as not to cause it to spew out smoke and deadly gases. Every morning during the winter of 1939–1940, even on the coldest days, the windows had to be opened to air the room out. We would also place heated bricks on our beds to warm them before we went to sleep. Our living space was small, but it was cozy, and the extra space provided by the second room was a welcome relief to all of us.

Our neighbourhood in Brussels was full of refugees, and we used an old building for community gatherings. Older people could play chess, talk and have tea with sandwiches for a nominal cost. The building also housed a youth centre staffed by refugee volunteers who taught flute and other musical instruments and organized games such as Ping-Pong. They also took us for outings to the surrounding forests on Sundays and holidays. The centre had a pleasant and communal atmosphere and gave the children of the refugees a necessary sanctuary and distraction. A colourful mix of people gathered there, making for a practical education in diversity, and I learned the customs and dialects of people from all over Europe, including Austria, southern Europe, Czechoslovakia, Hungary, Romania and the Balkans. It was also a politically opinionated group. The leaders of the youth group were mostly between twenty and thirty years old, most of them refugees from Austria. At the time, I found their German dialect very odd. Most of these leaders came from Austria's socialist party and had experience organizing and leading youth organizations, something they did very well, but in the process they attempted to sway us toward their leftist political world view. More useful was the way they tried to prepare us, physically and mentally, to survive this very difficult time in history.

With time we made some friends and acquaintances. There was a brother and sister from the family with whom we first stayed. The boy was my age and the girl was about sixteen. Their father was a cabinetmaker with a small shop of his own. We also met a tailor who had a workshop in the apartment where he lived with his wife, his son (who was my age) and his mother-in-law. The tailor had three sewing machines that he used for piecework he did for some factories.

I also met Harry Grunbaum and Manny Hausman and his brother, Bobbie, three of my former classmates from Leipzig. Harry, Manny and Bobbie arrived in Brussels after the German occupation, and all of them would survive the war. Harry was living with and working for his uncle, who was a tailor. Manny and Bobbie arrived by themselves and lived together on their own. In 1942 they succeeded in escaping to Venezuela by smuggling themselves over the Pyrenees mountain range into Spain, where their uncle in Madrid helped them cross the border into Portugal. From Portugal they journeyed by ship to Venezuela, where they had family. Manny and Bobbie were very resourceful boys, and I learned of their hair-raising adventures when I visited them and their families in Caracas, Venezuela, in the 1990s.

My father attended synagogue every Friday night and Saturday morning, and I accompanied him. One Saturday morning my father arranged for me to be called up to the Torah to recite a blessing and read a passage to compensate for the fact that I had missed my bar mitzvah on the night we crossed the German-Belgian border. My parents also implemented a traditional Shabbat dinner every Friday night. They had an acquaintance from Leipzig join us for these dinners, taking pity on this forty-five-year-old gentleman, as he was lonely and unable to speak or understand any French or Flemish.

I found Brussels to be much more beautiful than my first impression of it had suggested. The city had lush green parks, wide avenues and boulevards, and lovely neighbourhoods. I used to go out with other young people to indoor swimming pools, movies and the theatre. I also liked wandering aimlessly through the city streets. However, the local Jewish youth did not mix with us new Jewish refugees, and we were not integrated into the Jewish-Belgian community. Now, more than sixty years later, I think about the differences between life in Leipzig and in Brussels this way: In Leipzig the Jewish community was brought together by the threat to their very existence. Orthodox Jews cooperated with Reform Jews and other groups. The usual animosity that was felt by German Jews toward Eastern European Jewish immigrants was set aside, as survival was the only item on everyone's mind. In Brussels, this kind of struggle for survival was not yet known, therefore the established socio-economic and cultural divides between Jews were still entrenched. The refugees were not integrated into the Jewish community until 1944, when the lessons and losses of war were far more apparent and threatening. But, in the meantime, life continued with relative normalcy and routine, and I went to school until May 10, 1940.

The Earth Trembled

The general population underestimated the German threat in the months leading up to May 10, 1940, the date that Germany attacked the Western Front. The frequent flyovers by formations of the Belgian air force were not interpreted as serious military activities. There was a sense of confidence that the military action would be short-lived and that the German army would be defeated. But it did not take more than a day or two for the reality of the situation to become apparent and for worry to set in. The news was ominous, and our alarm deepened with every new communiqué, no matter how carefully worded. By May 14, 1940, there was a mass exodus, and the population started to evacuate major Belgian cities, including Brussels.

My parents, their gentleman friend and my sister and I went to the railway station on the night of May 15, where we were first told that a train would be arriving in an hour and then told that it would be delayed. There were no train tickets on sale, and there was a steady flow of people arriving at the station, overcrowding the platform. Finally, a train arrived, and it was announced that all those on the platform should board this train heading west. The crowd surged forward, everybody pushing, as no one wanted to be left behind. People were screaming, worried that they would lose their family and loved ones in the chaos of boarding.

We succeeded in staying together as we boarded the train. After a short wait, the train started to move out of the station in the direction of France. It moved extremely slowly, and we were told that the tracks had been badly damaged by bombing and that it was impossible to move any faster. After several hours the train could go no further, so we had to disembark and continue by foot. A river of people started to walk on the dusty country roads. It was extremely difficult to carry all the worldly possessions my parents had decided to bring with them — linens, comforters, towels, garments, shoes and all kinds of household goods — so some of our belongings had to be discarded immediately, yet it was still difficult to walk with the items we kept. We must have walked for hours. We had left Brussels in the morning and got off the train at noon. We arrived at the outskirts of Tournai, Belgium, near the French border, in the late afternoon when the sun was already low.

During the first few days of the war, while we were still in Brussels, we had watched German planes pass over the city while the anti-air defence shot at them. It was a spectacle that we tried not to miss, yet we never thought of seeking shelter during these episodes. This changed quickly.

As we walked the streets of Tournai, the sirens started to wail, and as usual we stared into the sky. We counted about fifteen German planes and observed the white clouds of anti-aircraft fire around them. But this time some of those planes started diving toward us, and we had a clear view of bombs being released! Everyone started running for shelter, and I was separated from my family and our friend in the chaos. There were hits all around us; the noise and screams were piercing. The dust was dense and it was impossible to see. The building I was in was hit and nearly destroyed. When the planes left and it was quiet, I came out from under the stairs, unhurt but completely black, covered in dust and debris. Many of the buildings around us were hit and totally destroyed. Everyone — soldiers and civilians alike — was trembling with fear after the raid was over.

I was told by a civil defence official to go to the air-raid shelter across the street, where I was lucky to find my parents, my sister and our family friend. Unfortunately, our friend became a suspect. The Belgian soldiers thought he was a German paratrooper and saboteur since he was not with his family and could not speak a word of French. My father had to convince these soldiers that, contrary to their belief, he was a refugee from the Nazis. He succeeded after hours of debating with them, but I don't know what happened to our friend after that.

We stayed overnight in the crowded shelter but did not experience any rest. My parents decided to repack and leave the majority of our belongings at the building with the shelter. Early in the morning we started to walk through the city of Tournai toward the French border. It was a difficult journey, climbing over the rubble of destroyed homes and seeing the cadavers of dead horses and dogs, as well as injured people who were staggering along. Suddenly, the sirens wailed again. This time we did not hesitate and ran for shelter. There was a group of people assigned to passive defence, and they were well organized, with someone stationed at every corner to direct people to nearby shelters. The one we arrived at had been prepared as a bomb shelter; it was a deep cellar with many rooms and double doors between these rooms. It also had some beds for injured people to lie on.

A short time after our arrival, the earth trembled underneath us, and everyone in the crowded shelter started to pray. The air was thick with dust and fumes. Some people attempted to leave the shelter before the sirens announced the end of the air raid, but they quickly returned. There was general panic and fear. When the raid was over and we finally emerged, it became apparent that the big tremor was a result of a direct hit to the building above us, which was completely flattened. The neighbourhood was also demolished.

Again we had to make our way over the rubble, encountering both the injured and their rescuers. As we tried to make our way to the French border, it slowly became apparent where we had to go. We followed the human stream as it merged into a large river of people heading in the same direction. We reached the border by the afternoon and became part of the masses of people who were stranded there. The rumour was that the French would not allow us to cross the border.

A column of Allied tanks was blocked from crossing the Belgian border and moving toward the front lines by the deluge of refugees in its path. German planes flew overhead, indiscriminately strafing civilians and military alike. Each time a German plane came near, people would chaotically disperse, screaming and running into the fields to try to find cover. The French finally relented and opened their border, and the refugees flowed through with difficulty, circumnavigating the craters and the stalled and abandoned vehicles.

It was nightfall by the time we reached the northern town of Douai, France. We immediately searched for a bomb shelter in which to pass the night. My parents understood how dangerous the bombing was and would not accept just any shelter. They kept looking until they found one they felt was strong enough to provide us with protection. Our shelter was large and well prepared, with strong tree trunks supporting the ceiling. Overnight there were a few alarms and bombs did fall but this time not in our immediate area. Needless to say, few in the shelter slept, including my family and me. Food and water was scarce, and we all were feeling the pangs of hunger, thirst and exhaustion.

In the morning, we continued our journey on foot in the direction of Arras, from where we would be able to catch a train to Paris. That night we arrived in Arras and boarded a freight train, which was supposed to journey to Paris in the morning. Since Arras was a railway junction, it was no surprise to us that the town was targeted by German bombers that very morning. People dispersed from the train cars and sought shelter beneath them. Unfortunately, we learned that some people had unknowingly and fatally selected shelter under a freight train that was loaded with ammunition. This train was selectively hit by the German bomber planes.

Our train moved out shortly after this raid was over. We were all extremely thirsty and hungry, but it was the thirst that was more unbearable. Despite our extreme discomfort, no one dared leave the train to forage for water in case the train moved ahead without them and they missed the chance to escape. We were also cautioned not to drink any water that we found as there was concern that the Germans may have poisoned water sources. It was rumoured that there was a German fifth column that had infiltrated France before the outbreak of the war. People were on edge, and the suspicion of German infiltration was so acute among the French population that it was considered dangerous to speak German for fear of being accused of being a German spy.

The train travelled at a snail's pace, stopping often; still, no one risked leaving, dreading the thought of being left behind. It took us two agonizing days to arrive in Paris. In total our travel time from Brussels to Paris took us one week, a distance that in peaceful times would have taken us only four hours. Today it takes less than two hours to travel from Brussels to Paris by train.

We arrived in Paris in the evening, completely exhausted, physically as well as mentally. We were filled with an ominous feeling of fear and anxiety, our nerves frayed. Fearing air attacks, we were startled by every noise. From the train station, we were directed to a Jewish centre, where the staff were caring and compassionate. They let us wash up and then provided us with food and drink. They then gave us lists, complete with addresses and telephone numbers, of people who were expecting relatives or friends to arrive from the east. The staff also registered all of our personal details, and hotel and restaurant vouchers were given to all of the refugees. Later, as I recalled our experience at the centre, I was impressed with this phenomenal display of human compassion we encountered in a time of extreme distress.

We arrived at our assigned hotel very late at night, and were happy to learn that we'd been provided with a large room. The next day we walked a block or two to the restaurant to enjoy our lunch and dinner vouchers.

On our second morning in Paris, we received a surprise visit from my father's cousin. We knew that he lived in Paris, but for some reason my parents did not have his address. Our cousin had been given our address by the Jewish committee, as they had carefully recorded all the refugees' information as they arrived. We were invited to his modest home on Rue du Faubourg-du-Temple, in the middle of Paris. It was similar to many immigrants' homes in Brussels, serving not only as a place of shelter but also as a workshop. He subcontracted work in the leather industry, making luxury ladies' handbags from crocodile and other expensive leathers. His son, about ten years old at the time, became my guide to this Paris neighbourhood.

One day, as my family and I wandered the streets of Paris, we entered a large department store. As my mother crossed paths with a woman who was slightly older than her, they both looked intently at each other but then kept walking. All of a sudden, both turned around and yelled each other's names — this woman was my mother's cousin, and they had not seen each other for more than a decade! We all went to her home, another very modest place centrally located in a Jewish district of Paris. Her husband was missing at the time, though I don't remember why. She also had a daughter, who must have been in her early twenties, and her daughter's boyfriend lived with her along with one of his friends. All of them were occupied with the assembly of radios on a piecework basis. The kitchen was strewn with radio parts, and they were all busy welding and packing the finished products. I was awed by the sight of what I considered to be, at that time, a high-tech product. They worked while they talked with my parents. Everyone was happy to have found each other, but the discussion quickly turned to the more sombre topic of the reality of the war. There was no encouraging news. We talked about leaving Paris for a safer haven in the south of France; the younger people in the room had a plan to start their journey by bicycle.

To me Paris was a welcoming city, and I had an experience that reinforced my idea that, overall, the people there were decent. I enjoyed riding the metro, and one morning I was travelling on it on my own. I do not recall where I was going, but on this particular trip I fainted, and when I came to, I was on the terrace of a café with several people surrounding me. As they continued to revive me, they urged me to drink water. After a while I felt my strength return, and I stood up to leave, but the people insisted on sending me home in a taxi that they paid for.

One day, when we returned to our hotel, my parents were presented with a note ordering my father to appear at the Polish army compound operated by the Polish government-in-exile. I vividly recall the anxious discussions between my parents about this order, and their decision to follow it. We believed that he was being mobilized to the Polish Armed Forces in the West, which had joined the Allied forces.

My next distinct memory takes place around the end of May 1940, when refugees and Parisians were told to leave Paris because the Germans were approaching. We were assigned a railway station to meet at and were ordered onto a train travelling west to Rennes, in Brittany. At Rennes we were supplied with food and water. I do not recall any hardship on this involuntary journey. The next station on our trip was Vannes, close to the Atlantic coast. At Vannes we disembarked. The train was filled with refugees, mostly of Polish descent, and there were miners from the coal-mining regions of Alsace-Lorraine and Ardennes. Several buses were waiting for us at the train station, each with a different destination. The one that my mother, my sister and I boarded arrived in Port Arthur, two kilometres northwest of the village of Pluméliau, which was north of Vannes and away from the coast.

Our entire bus of approximately sixty people was assigned to a farm building that was divided into dormitories for men and women. Some supplies were handed out, and we all started to settle in. The dormitories had small wooden beds with straw mattresses. There was some space around each bed where we could keep our belongings.

With time people started to build some shelves and organize their lives in these small compartments. There was a common kitchen area for food preparation where each family or extended family could prepare their own meals. We met a Jewish man from Brussels and a Jewish couple of Hungarian descent who were also from Brussels. Life was bearable but not pleasant. Given the situation, no one complained, but we were filled with worry and anxiety.

We spent the first few days on the farm acclimatizing and exploring our surroundings. The owner of the farm, who lived across the street, owned several farms. He cultivated his farms using the *métayage* system, a kind of sharecropping, which involved the farmer hiring workers, *métayers*, who cultivated the land and received a share of the produce. The war changed this system, as the *métayers* were mobilized for battle, leaving the farmer to work the land by himself with the help of farmhands. As time passed, some of the other refugees and I started to help the farmer run his farm. He had two daughters and a son who was two or three years younger than I was. While I was there I built a terrific relationship with the farmer and his family.

We arrived at the farm at the end of May or beginning of June, when hay-harvesting season was under way. My initiation into farm work involved preparing the hay: turning it over for drying, raking it into long narrow rows that the baling machines would gather into heaps, and loading it onto ox-driven wagons, which were then unloaded into the barn. All this work with hay triggered hay fever, which I continued to suffer from throughout my life. But at the time I liked the work; it made me feel like one of the adults, though I was only just under fourteen. The wheat harvest was later in the season, and since the farmer had by then grown fond of me, he allowed me to help him guide the horse on his wheat-cutting machine. My responsibility was to steer the horse in the right direction while the farmer ensured that the wheat entered his old wheat-cutting machine properly. Many times I also helped churn the butter, which involved

turning the hand-driven separator for many hours, a very difficult
task for me given my young age.

I worked steadily for long hours every day and enjoyed very hearty
meals with the farmer and his farmhands. The work was back-breaking, and at night I suffered from aches and pains to the point where
I sometimes could not sleep. But I resumed my work each morning
with no complaint; it was a matter of pride for me. The farmer must
have appreciated my work and reliability because he gave my mother,
sister and me an extra room near his home, so we had much more
privacy than any of the other refugees. He also supplied my mother
with milk, butter, cheese, vegetables and fruits and me with some
pocket money every week. When there was a day without work, the
farmer took me with him to help run errands in the village, where he
would stop at the local bistro to meet his friends for a drink. At other
times, when farm work was not pressing, I joined a group of youths,
and we rode our bikes to a river not far from the farm. The landscape
was very scenic, and it was a perfect bathing spot for us. I had free
use of the farmer's daughter's bicycle when I wanted it and so was
able to explore the surroundings, going into Pontivy and Pluméliau
whenever there was no work to be done.

In the meantime, the Allied forces had been defeated, and we saw
some of the British Air Force retreating southward toward Vannes
in trucks that also carried parts of planes. The British troops looked
very tired; the soldiers were slumped in the backs of the trucks. Several hours later we saw German soldiers ride through on their motorcycles on the same route, and right after them, columns of German
trucks. It was very disheartening to see this, and we were filled with
worry and anxiety. Several days later the Germans positioned themselves in Pluméliau. On a subsequent visit to the village, I observed
the installation of anti-aircraft guns on top of the church tower and
German trucks parked along the roads.

Shortly after the Germans had installed themselves at Pluméliau,
I became very ill with hay fever. The doctor had me admitted for ob-

servation to the village infirmary, an eight-bed room at the back of an enclosed yard with a nurse on duty. As I improved I was allowed to go out into the street, so I would go and stand beside the German trucks, where there were always German soldiers conversing. Not knowing, of course, that I spoke German fluently, they ignored me while I listened to their conversations intently. I heard these soldiers talking about how they were worried about their families, as the Rhineland was suffering from Allied bombings, and about how difficult transportation was now. Hearing this lifted my spirits very much. I realized that the Germans were encountering losses and that the war was not over yet.

A Community in Peril

In September 1940 we were told by the French government to return to our homes in Brussels. Transportation by bus and railway was provided free, so we went back to Brussels together with our new friends from the farm — the Jewish man from Brussels and the Jewish-Hungarian couple.

The reality in Brussels was harsh. All financial assistance for refugees had been terminated; no unemployment funding or subsidies were provided any longer. There was a shortage of food, with long lines for every kind of necessity. Food and clothing were strictly rationed and could be acquired only with our allotment of food stamps or ration cards, a system that affected everyone.

We returned to our apartment and tried without success to repossess the belongings that we'd left in the bomb shelter in Tournai when we were fleeing to France. My mother decided that investing in legal fees to have our possessions returned was throwing good money after bad, and the idea was abandoned.

It wasn't possible for me to return to school as we had an urgent need for money for food and rent, and during this time of turmoil and trouble finding work was very difficult. My sister did return to school as she was only seven years old and there was nothing else for her to do at that young age. My mother did her best to make money and resumed her dressmaking; however, it was difficult to get decent remuneration when everyone else was also suffering under the tough economic conditions brought on by war, and especially difficult for us as refugees with no previous connections in the city. The gentleman we had met at the farmhouse in Brittany had a fur store close to where we were living, and in the first, most difficult month, he brought us food he had purchased on the black market. This helped to alleviate some of our distress.

I would travel to the outskirts of Brussels to purchase whatever food I could from farmers and then sell half of it or more on the black market in order to cover my costs, and in this way I earned enough to feed us. After a while I landed a job as a furrier's apprentice, but this lasted only three weeks. Then I was hired as a hairdresser's apprentice, which also lasted only two or three weeks. Pay was always extremely meagre. My mother made ready-to-wear dresses to sell in a store that her new business partner owned. I worked in the store, but this venture was not successful either. Earning a little money standing in lines for people or looking for a job was my depressing daily occupation for a short while. Then I found a job in the leather industry making ladies' purses and wallets. I started as an apprentice and worked there for two or three months.

I later found a better-paying job at a large leather goods factory, where I was taught many useful skills such as cutting. The boss involved himself in every task of production, no matter how menial or dirty, even though he had about fifty employees. Overall, his example influenced my work ethic and way of thinking in later years. He gave me the opportunity to earn extra money by having me deliver to customers that he knew would tip me well, and he had me sell some of his merchandise on the black market. I would arrive at work at seven in the morning to open the shop and put coal in the ovens, so that by eight they were hot. I was also the last to leave at seven or eight at night. I was working seventy to eighty hours a week and earning substantially more than I had been. My employer began to trust me and invited me to eat with him, a significant benefit at that time. I was also allowed to take the bicycle used for errands home with me for my own use overnight. My employment with this man eased our struggle for survival a great deal.

My long workday meant that during the winter months, I left home in the dark and returned home in the dark. Complete darkness was enforced on the city as an air defence measure, so that enemy planes could not use light to identify targets. Some big windows and display windows were painted dark blue to keep light from inside homes and stores from reflecting onto the street. We had to use battery-operated flashlights in order to navigate our way through the streets, and we limited the light by covering the flashlights with our hands. We learned to recognize the engine noises of the various English warplanes, like the Lancasters, which were long-range British bombers. The anti-aircraft fire was often already in action as I returned from work, and I could recognize the sound of spent shells from the anti-aircraft weapons falling to earth. The British were not bombing Brussels at that time, but there was an incessant fear of being bombed.

One of the other employees at my workplace, a young man two or three years older than me, befriended me. He invited me to play Ping-Pong at some cafés on Sundays. He would pay for me, and we would play for hours. He was a far better player than I was. Eventually he invited me to join a large and diverse group of people on Sunday outings. It took me a while to understand that these young people were an illegal group of Trotsky followers. Slowly I was introduced to discussions of Leon Trotsky's ideology, which opposed Stalin's authoritarian approach in favour of a more democratic rule that allowed for a range of ideas.

One Sunday, as I was taking a stroll, I came across a demonstration of about a thousand people next to the opera house. There were German *Feldgendarmerie*, field gendarmes or military police, in command cars in the middle of this huge crowd. The crowd was jeering loudly at the Germans. Suddenly I heard a German officer tell his driver to drive into the crowd with force. The crowd reacted by

threatening violence and was close to overturning the German vehicles. The *Feldgendarmes* pulled out their guns and started to shoot
into the air, and the crowd dispersed frantically.

~

I believe that our greater difficulties started around 1942. In October
1940, the Germans had established a policy that all Jews needed to
register with the Belgian authorities and have their identification
cards marked. And in May 1942 the Jews were required to identify
themselves by wearing a yellow Star of David on their clothing. One
day, as I was walking through the Jewish district, I witnessed a young
German officer stop an elderly Jew with a long beard. Without any
provocation, the German officer forcefully pulled and tore at the elderly man's beard, verbally abused him and then struck and kicked
him. The poor gentleman was visibly hurt, and the officer seemed to
enjoy his pain and grief. A crowd formed around this scene, and the
German officer attempted, unsuccessfully, to order the crowd to disperse. Once he realized that the crowd was not going to budge despite
his panicked orders, the officer left. That crowd of people likely saved
the elderly Jew's life. As I had witnessed the events of Kristallnacht in
1938, this type of brutality was not new to me, but it certainly was to
the Belgians.

In 1942 I continued to sell my boss's products on the black market,
making a lucrative living for both of us. I learned about the inner
workings of the market and earned the trust of many people who
sought me out to buy and sell merchandise for them. For my remaining time in Belgium, the black market was my main occupation, and
the money I earned became essential to my family's survival. From
these savings I used six thousand francs — a substantial amount of
money at that time — to acquire false identity papers, which meant
we didn't have to wear the yellow Star of David. I was able to give my
mother an additional ten thousand francs, which helped us survive
the very hard times ahead.

Because of my false identity papers, I also did not need to abide by the curfew that had been implemented in August 1941, which required Jews to be off the streets by 8:00 p.m. On one occasion I was stopped by a Belgian fascist who questioned me and did not believe that I was not Jewish despite my identity papers and my forceful denial of being Jewish. He finally succumbed, returned my papers to me and let me go; perhaps he did not wish to risk being ridiculed by his friends.

In the spring of 1942, the Germans issued summonses to a portion of the Jewish population for forced labour, *Arbeitseinsatz*, enforcing it with draconian measures. If a Jew failed to show up for work camp, the Germans would forcefully conscript all the Jews who lived at that address, sometimes taking all the residents of the building. The Germans also deceived the Jewish population with fake postcards that were supposedly sent by family members who had been taken to work camps, with descriptions of their arrival at the work camps in northern France as bearable and not too harsh. In reality, the Jews who showed up for forced labour at this time were deported to Auschwitz. It was a well-organized deception, and most Jews fell for it.

My family was part of a minority of Jews who understood early on that the Germans had malevolent intentions. We attempted to dispel the myth that they were only taking a select few of us to the work camps, and without success we tried to persuade the Jewish community not to comply with the work orders and to escape detection by hiding. Some Jewish community members were violently opposed to this approach. Many felt disgust at the possibility of hiding, when the consequence was that others would be taken away in their stead. Our argument for non-compliance was not accepted, and those of us who held this view were marginalized by the community and looked upon as immoral criminals. It was very painful that our community rejected us and was not yet able to see the inherent peril in the German policies.

Our friend from Brittany was a leader in the Jewish community.

He was one of the few to hold the view that the entire Jewish community of Belgium was in peril. He came to us one morning and advised us to flee, as he had knowledge that I was to receive a work order shortly. The Germans' brutal strategy, and its acceptance by some members of the Jewish community, was tragic and ironic. I now had to hide not only from the Germans, as false papers were never a guarantee of safety, but also from our own community members, who believed that my mobilization would save some "innocent" Jewish community members. The German deception was very successful, making it easy for them to arrest and gather Jews with minimal effort.

We went into hiding with several Jewish people who were not yet subject to the German work camp orders and with Spanish Christians I knew from the black market. The Spaniards were professional smugglers who made their living smuggling products between Belgium and France. It was not unusual for one or more of their family members to be in jail for smuggling offences. The Spaniards showed compassion for our cause, and with the help of some money (I can't recall how much) they arranged a strategy to smuggle me into France.

Since June 1940 France had been split between the German-occupied north and French-controlled south. The French government had relocated to Vichy and was headed by Marshal Philippe Pétain, and at the time I was preparing to leave Belgium, we erroneously considered Pétain's Vichy France to be free.

The Art of Deception

At sixteen, I left my mother and sister and set off for France, equipped with false identity papers stating that my age was nineteen. We believed that if I presented myself as older it would be easier for me to find work. I was accompanied on my trip by one of the Spanish smugglers and his girlfriend, but we always kept a distance between us so that we wouldn't implicate each other if one of us was arrested.

At the Belgian-French border there was a thorough security check, and my identity papers were scrutinized by the German border police. The officer inspecting my papers addressed me in German, but I pretended not to understand him. When he ordered me to remove my hat, I again feigned incomprehension. He then knocked my hat off my head with a flick of his finger. Staying calm, I turned around and picked my hat up from the ground, pretending to be confused about what was happening. Finally, the officer returned my false identity papers and waved me off. I was relieved and delighted that I was able to calmly withstand my first test in the art of deception, as many more tests of my nerves were yet to come.

Shortly after our arrival at the railway station in Paris, the French security officers moved in on the Spanish couple and checked their belongings, but they were unable to find any of the smuggled goods they were carrying. The couple was released and allowed to depart; I followed closely behind them. Later they helped me rent a small room in a hotel not far from their tiny apartment. The hotel was located close to the Les Halles district, where wholesale foods were bought and sold. It was an extremely dense, noisy and colourful area of Paris.

About three weeks passed before we left for the so-called *zone libre*, the free zone in the southeastern part of the country, which was controlled by the Vichy government. In the meantime, I started exploring the immediate surroundings of the Les Halles district. I vividly remember being propositioned by prostitutes several times and then cursed for not returning their hungry attention. I attempted to locate my cousins. I could not find my father's cousin, but I found my mother's cousin at the same address she had been at in 1940 when I met her with my family. She was alone at that time. Since I did not wear the yellow Star of David and she had to, I didn't dare walk beside her, and we would walk on opposite sides of the street when we were out together. After the war I made inquiries regarding her whereabouts but could not find her or her daughter. I was unable to locate my father's cousin and his family either.

I spent my days exploring Paris. Yet I was aware of and experienced first-hand the dangers that existed at the time. I once saw a crowd of people gather in the street in front of me. Suspecting an identity check, I looked around and noticed some men standing behind the checkpoint, observing the reactions of people and specifically looking for anyone who was trying to avoid the checkpoint. It was clear that this was a trap. If I turned around to avoid the checkpoint, I would be arrested. So I approached bravely, feeling my heart beating intensely in my chest, and showed my papers. I was released and once again felt enormous relief.

I enjoyed walking along both sides of the Seine River. At that time you were able to walk right along the riverbanks, which were later turned into highways. Occasionally I went swimming in the river pools, which were surrounded by fixed floating barges that had change rooms, restaurants and restrooms. The parks and the whole area around the Louvre and along the Champs-Élysées were fascinating places for me. I sometimes wandered far along the river, all the way to the busy harbour area where the automobile factories were located.

The day came when the Spaniards arranged for my transport to Vierzon, a border town between German-occupied France and the *zone libre*. Again, the couple and I rode the same train but kept our distance from each other. When we arrived at Vierzon, we decided to leave all of our belongings in a locker at the train station. This turned out to be a very lucky decision.

The couple then hired a taxi, which dropped us off somewhere close to the Cher River, which was part of the demarcation line between the occupied zone and the free zone. We continued by foot on an unpaved country road, with me several metres behind the couple. After about a half-hour we stopped at some bushes and trees where I was told to stay so that they could walk ahead and explore the possibility of crossing the river. I hid in the bushes looking out to the river and observed the brush along the riverbank about fifty metres ahead. I lay there feeling anxious and tense. After a while I noticed an armed German gendarme with a German Shepherd dog appear from the dense brush of the riverbank and realized that the couple had been caught. Immediately I rolled into a ditch behind me and hid behind a very large tree. My green and khaki clothing had been deliberately chosen to camouflage me. My heart pounded sharply in my chest as I lay behind the tree, listening to the footsteps of the oncoming party. I could clearly hear the panting of the dog as they passed about two metres from me. I stopped breathing for what felt like a very long time, hoping that the dog would not detect me. I was relieved to hear the footsteps become fainter.

But my problems were not over. I still had to cross the river, with no guide to help me. I slowly made my way closer to the river to where the bushes were densest. On the way I saw a field labourer and tried to get some information from him, but he refused to talk to me, probably scared of the repercussions. Once in the river, I began to swim frantically to the other side, afraid that I'd be discovered by a German gendarme and get a bullet in my back. The river currents were strong and I had to swim hard. During my panicked swim, I lost nearly all of my remaining possessions and was left with little more than the clothes on my back.

When I reached the other side, I ran into the forest. I undressed and wrung the water out of my clothing as best I could. It was now late in the afternoon, and I was cold, wet and shivering. I wanted to distance myself from the border, and so I had to pass under a bridge, where I noticed another German *Feldgendarme*. Once more, I could feel my heart beating intensely, but he did not notice me. At a cross-road I met some people who directed me to a shelter for refugees where I received some food and a straw bed for the night. What I didn't know was that the shelter was controlled by the French gendarmerie. Two French gendarmes came early in the morning, waited for me to have some breakfast and then took me into custody.

I was taken to the police headquarters and peppered with an exhaustive string of questions, though without intimidation or threats. The two officers questioning me concentrated on my identity papers: my name, my parents' identities and occupations, the identities of my other family members, my school, schoolmates, teachers and the reasons that I left home. During the questioning, I was presented with an offer to join the French Foreign Legion (FFL), the implication being that if I agreed to join, there would be no further questions. I was not prepared to answer the barrage of questions thrown at me, and it became clear to me that my identity papers had caused suspicion. After what seemed to be one or more hours of endless questioning, I finally admitted that my identity papers were false. When their offer to join the FFL was repeated, I was confused as to how to respond and hesitated as I puzzled over their real intentions. Finally, I agreed to join, but I also revealed that my true age was only sixteen. Both interrogators said that sixteen was too young to be in the FFL. I was returned to the refugee shelter without my identity papers.

Two years later I learned that the German *Feldgendarmes* who had intercepted the Spanish couple had taken them to the police station, where they were interrogated for several hours by different German officials about their walk along the demarcation line. Both of them, in separate rooms, maintained that their walk was just a romantic one through the wilderness. They were then both inspired to tell the Germans that all their belongings had been left at the railway station locker (the suitcase in the locker was mine) and insisted that this was proof that they had no intention of crossing the border but rather had intended to return to the station and continue their journey back to northern France. A *Feldgendarme* went to the train station with them to verify the suitcase story. When the suitcase was found where they claimed they had left it, the German released the couple and rationalized their strange behaviour as being that of the "crazy" French.

I was now in a refugee shelter with no identity papers, along with eight or so other people in the same predicament. We were all free to move around the perimeter of the shelter, but having no papers made it dangerous to venture out. We were all cordial toward one another, but not knowing or trusting each other completely, our relationships remained formal only. After several days the French gendarmes returned for me. They brought me to the station and provided me with a *laissez-passer*, a travel document that could be used for one-way travel to a specific location. The *laissez-passer* I received was for a trip to Lyon, to Les Compagnons de France, the Companions of France, an organization dedicated to assisting the abandoned and orphaned youth that the war had produced. Two other inhabitants at the shelter received the same type of *laissez-passer* to Lyon. I paid for my travel expenses from my reserve, aware that I had to carefully budget the money I had to make it last until I found employment. During the trip our identity papers were checked several times, and when we arrived at Lyon, we parted ways.

I arrived at the address I was given at night and was assigned a wooden bed with a straw mattress in a large dormitory where other boys were already settled for the night. Every boy had a bed and some shelf space beside the bed. The rest of our belongings were stored under our beds. I was awakened with the rest of the boys at six in the morning. At seven there was a salute to the flag and an inspection for cleanliness, and then a simple breakfast was served. Some of the boys left for work, others left to search for work. The rules at the dormitory were very simple: We all had to keep our bed and surrounding areas neat and clean. Some of the boys were assigned chores in the dormitory, and the rest of us were not permitted to return to the dormitory until after five in the afternoon. At six, supper was served. I was summoned to the office the morning after my arrival, and the rules were explained to me in detail. That day I strolled the streets of Lyon to get acquainted with the city with the goal of finding work and my own accommodations. I wrote to the Spanish couple and asked them to forward my belongings to me. They did this promptly, at which point I learned that they had been freed and were safe.

I started to search for employment. I entered a drugstore and spoke with a woman who worked there. I had to purchase a toothbrush, toothpaste, shoe polish and shoelaces. She asked me where I was from, and I told her I had come from Belgium and that I was residing at the nearby Companions of France dormitory and was looking for work. She kindly invited me to dinner with her husband that night and several nights after that.

Wandering the streets of Lyon one rainy day, I was caught in a torrential rainfall. I sought shelter on a covered porch with several other people, including a priest. He approached me and started a friendly conversation. In my naivety, not yet understanding that the southern French were not as free as I thought they were, I informed this man that I was a refugee from Belgium and before that from Germany. He listened attentively and wished me well when he left the porch. When the rain stopped, I returned to the dormitory. I was immediately called into the office, where a young man advised me that I was no longer permitted to roam the streets. I was extremely surprised and asked why. The young man then explained to me that southern France was not completely free and that the Vichy government was collaborating with the Germans, which meant that I could be arrested and deported. Clearly, the priest had spoken to him. He gave me an address and urged me to go there immediately. When I arrived I recognized it to be a Jewish organization for refugees. Two people spoke to me and advised me to collect my belongings in order to join a transport of youth that was to be smuggled to Switzerland. I understood the risks involved in remaining in France and was very happy to follow their advice. When I returned to the refugee shelter, I was again called to the office and informed that plans had been changed; I was to travel that same evening to another destination, which was not specified to me.

I was suspicious, so I ran back to the couple from the Jewish organization, and I was reassured that the new travel plans were legitimate. I met the young man who was to be in charge of our journey. Joining us was Wolodia, an eighteen-year-old former Soviet soldier who had escaped from a German prison camp close to the German-French border along with several French prisoners.

The man who was in charge of me and Wolodia had travel papers for us, and he made certain that he was in charge of all of our interactions, including the train ticket purchases and meal orders. This was especially necessary since Wolodia could not speak any French. We had to change trains several times on our journey, eventually arriving in Toulouse, where we were able to enjoy a meal at a restaurant. The large harvest of beans in this region meant that most of my meals during this time were made of beans: bean salad, bean soup and various types of bean purée. We continued our trip by bus, changing once or twice before we arrived at our destination, the village of Cazaubon, in the southwest of France.

Respite in the South

From the village we walked about two kilometres to a place between Cazaubon and Barbotan. We walked along a shady and dusty country road lined with trees, which led to the impressive Château du Bégué. This was to be my home for about one year. Of all my memories, I cherish my experiences at this château the most. Wolodia and I were introduced to Victor Vermont (whose real name was Vila Glasberg), the manager of the château. Vermont had been in the French army, the F F L, I believe, in Indochina, before World War II. The château was a part of the organization Amitié Chretiénne, Christian Fellowship, which saved many refugees and was co-founded by Victor's brother, Father Alexandre Glasberg.

Abbé Glasberg, a Ukrainian immigrant and Jewish-born convert to Catholicism, was a renowned vicar of Notre-Dame de Saint-Alban, one of the poorest parishes in the suburbs of Lyon. A high-ranking priest in the Catholic Church of France, the Abbé had many contacts and assistants. He cooperated effectively with all the Jewish organizations and was responsible for saving many Jewish lives. He was fluent in Russian, German and French and also spoke Yiddish and Hebrew. He enjoyed sitting with the youth in our group and listening to old Yiddish and Hebrew songs. It was always an event when he visited.

I quickly became acclimatized to life in Château du Bégué. There must have been a hundred people there when I arrived. Later I counted about one hundred and fifty occupants. We were a diverse assortment of people ranging in age from sixteen to sixty, including Jews from all over Europe — Poland, France, Germany, Czechoslovakia, the Netherlands, Austria — as well as non-Jews, Spanish democrats, a Spanish pilot and Germans who had fought with the International Brigades in Spain (our crazy cook was one). I later learned that there were also two German parliamentarians who had opposed Hitler as he rose to power and then fled to France in 1933 after he was appointed chancellor.

Our landlords were Count Henri d'André and his wife, Countess Simone. They owned many properties and had farmers working their land as *métayers*. Mr. d'André was also a high-ranking official in a French petroleum company and was responsible for the distribution of the precious commodity of vehicle fuel. Our landlords had two sons at the time, aged three and twelve. I visited both of them in 1995 and expressed my thanks for their parents' deeds.[1]

On the first floor of the Château du Bégué there was a big communal dining room and kitchen. Mr. Vermont's office was also on the first floor, along with the dormitory for the younger boys. The second and third floors had bedrooms. There were also what we called annexes, dwellings that were attached to the château. Most of them had not been completed, though one of them, which was directly attached to the château, had been finished and served as our recreation room. Behind this area was a laundry room.

There were people from every walk of life at the château: a couple of piano players; a writer who later became an antique dealer; a shoemaker of Jewish-German descent who repaired our shoes using old tires as soles. There were also those who had been immensely wealthy and had difficulty adjusting to our new community-based lifestyle.

---

1 The family was honoured by Yad Vashem as Righteous Among the Nations in 2006. See http://db.yadvashem.org/righteous/family.html?language=en&itemId=5774194

There was an ambitious seventeen-year-old named Ady Steg who was determined not to lose at any sport, game or intellectual debate. After the war Ady would become a professor of medicine and the surgeon for General de Gaulle and President Mitterand. Professor Steg also became a leader of the French Jewish community. Ady was there with his older brother, Henry, and his younger sister, Albertine, who was about my age. They were my close companions during this period, and after the war we stayed in contact and met several times.

Another outstanding young man in our midst was Alfred Frisch, who was twelve years my senior. Every week Alfred would put together a summary of the news based on information he was able to gather from radio broadcasts and from several newspapers. Later, Alfred became like a surrogate older brother. He directed me in my reading and watched over me, making sure that I did not make foolish mistakes, and he gave me money when I desperately needed it. After the war I regularly visited with him and his wife, Lilian, in Paris.

There were also two brothers, Leo and Harry Paul, who had a big influence on me. I remember Leo telling me that he hoped that Château du Bégué would be an education for me. Leo was very knowledgeable about agriculture; he oversaw our food production at the château and was responsible for ensuring that there were enough fruits and vegetables to feed 150 of us. His brother, Harry, was physically strong and sometimes impatient and aggressive toward others. He was not an intellectual, but he was very good at woodwork and other physical work. However, he had no compassion for those who could not do hard physical labour when they were tired or did not have the strength. He had been part of a Polish unit in Norway when the Germans invaded that country, and he claimed that he had been torpedoed and rescued from drowning several times. Many of his stories of war were rife with cruelty and violence.

Mr. Joseph Constant was an able sculptor and painter who specialized in animal sculptures and paintings of landscapes. He also wrote some books in French, one of which I had the pleasure of later reading. He spoke many languages, including his mother tongue of

Russian. Born in Russia, he immigrated to Palestine in 1919, lived in Egypt for a short period and then immigrated to France in 1923. After he returned to Israel in 1950, I helped him with his art exposition at the Tel Aviv Museum of Art. His wife was also a sculptor, working mostly in clay. I was surprised to hear in the welcoming speeches of his art exposition in Tel Aviv that he had been well known to the Israeli artist community from his earlier stay in Palestine.

Mr. Chino was a teacher and educator from the Jewish ORT network, the Organization for Rehabilitation through Training. He was also an accomplished woodworker and made excellent furniture, doors and windows. I had the privilege of working with him on several projects for our landlord. While at the château Mr. Chino mounted and directed two dramatic productions, also designing the stage. It was my job to manage the production of the show. The villagers were invited, and it was an exceptional success.

It wasn't always easy for such a multitude of people to get along peacefully, but in general we were able to at the château. Since there were many young single boys and girls, romance was frequent and some lasting unions developed, though of course breakups occurred as well. In such a close society, we all knew what was going on in each other's lives, and the rumour mills did not rest.

Mr. Vermont assembled us from time to time to allow us to vent our problems and to instill in us, and especially in the younger members of our group, morals, ambitions and hope for the future. One of his principles was that we were each responsible for our own actions and should not hide behind excuses. His other favourite concept was that there is no such thing as demeaning work. He believed that all honest work was honourable as long as it was done well.

In general we worked all day, every day. Everyone was assigned tasks on a rotating basis. We planted corn and beans, attended to our large fruit and vegetable crops and cleared fields so that we could plant more crops. One of the many chores we were assigned was gathering and splitting firewood. We often had to obtain permission from the local farmers to gather wood from their land. On one occasion we arrived at a farm to gather firewood and were greeted by the farmer's teenage son. The boy asked his father if we were Jews and when the farmer answered that we were, the boy then asked, "How so? They look like everyone else." This incident only confirmed to us that the German propaganda that demonized us was being widely spread.

Many of the residents of the château worked at other farms or vineyards as well. Sometimes a group of us was dispatched to a farm or a municipality for a specific project. Our labour was seen as a great help in the region, given that much of the population was absent, having been taken as prisoners of war. The mayor and his staff supported our presence and our employment. My first outside job was at one of the vineyards, where I helped make wine. My experience was tough because of the constant rain. It was difficult to move around in the thick mud wearing the wooden shoes we had been given and carrying baskets that were heavy with the harvest. I was unaccustomed to this back-breaking work, though the winemaking itself was an interesting process. The grapes were placed in a hand-operated grinding machine where the juices were extracted; the remnants were then transferred to a hand-operated pressing apparatus — a large screw that was turned using long levers so as to press out the maximum amount of juice; then the produce was transferred to a hydraulic press that was operated by hand like a pump. The juice was then placed into large barrels for fermenting, after which it was transferred several times to smaller barrels. With each transfer, the debris at the bottom of the barrels was discarded.

The local farmers usually treated us well. They fed us and insisted that we drink their wine. It was almost impossible to refuse their offers to drink, and I often suffered from the after-effects. The farmers also insisted on providing us with wine to quench our thirst after working in the hot sun and the dusty fields. They thought of plain water as an insult to our efforts. And so we suffered even further from dehydration. I recall one incident when three of us were sent to work on a farm about ten kilometres from the château. We walked there and were going to sleep there overnight so that we could harvest the corn the next day. It was a very hot day, and the fields were dry and dusty. We had to drink, and yet we could not convince the lady of the farm to give us water. Instead, we received an abundance of wine. After we finished our job, we were invited to a very generous dinner with copious amounts of wine. We then had to walk the ten kilometres back home to the château. The woman probably felt some remorse at sending us away in the dark in such a drunken state, as she hurriedly came after us on her bicycle to make sure we were okay and not lying somewhere on the forest floor.

Another person I developed a relationship with at the château was Stanislav Besborodko. Stany was a thirty-year-old Russian-born Jew, an excellent salesman, a charmer and a catch for Marlene, a slightly older widow from Luxembourg with twin twelve-year-old daughters. Stany was fluent in Russian, German and French. His negotiating skills were superlative, so he was assigned the role of making food purchases — eggs, animal products, milk and bread. He had a warm heart and was a good friend to Alfred Frisch during and after the war. Later, Stany married Marlene and set up a mirror factory. I met with him and his family several times in Paris and when they visited Israel, where Marlene's family owned some hotels. In 1967, when I visited Paris, I stayed with Stany for one week, and he was kind enough to take us for a tour through the Bois de Boulogne park and other places of interest.

Stany looked after me and taught me how to buy supplies for the château. I would bicycle to other farms to collect eggs, beans, chickens, butter, cheese and so on. At nearly every farm I was invited to join them for lunch or dinner if it was mealtime or close to mealtime. If it was not, I was offered a glass or two of wine. This meant that over the course of a day I had to drink many glasses of wine. As I returned to the château in the evenings, I was frequently found staggering unsteadily off my bike! One day I had to start my rounds very early and arrived at a farmhouse at six in the morning. The farmer, pitying me for riding through the extreme cold, offered me a soup bowl filled with equal portions of Armagnac brandy and milk. My protestations went unheard. It was the cultural way to show kindness and respect.

Wolodia, my young Russian friend, became an example to me of extreme narrow-mindedness. One day when Stany mentioned Trotsky, Wolodia lurched toward him and grabbed his throat, assaulting him. Once, when Mr. d'André was driving away, Wolodia raised his hands as though he were holding a gun and gestured as if to shoot Mr. d'André, making shotgun noises and exclaiming, "Capitalist!" His actions were disturbing and I believe a result of his limited, absolutist educational background. In early 1944 he was tragically killed by German fire in a battle between the French Resistance and the Germans.

In November 1942 the Germans occupied the *zone libre*. At some point a decision was made to dig a tunnel from the château to a site bordered by thick vegetation to create an escape route from the château should it be raided by the Germans. When I visited in 1995 and asked Mr. d'André's son about it, he led me to that tunnel, telling me that it had been used to store illegal arms after I left. After the German occupation, the laneway leading to the château was guarded permanently, and an electric bell was installed to warn of any approaching danger. We all had to take our turns at guard duty. Everyone was provided with instructions for their assigned escape routes. However, on our trial runs, our escape plans did not seem to work so smoothly. We all carried false papers indicating that we were French Christians and were taught to behave like dimwits when encountering police or Germans. We hoped that this would prevent the Germans from suspecting our identities.

Abbé Glasberg visited the château several times, usually accompanied by Mrs. Nina and Mrs. Nino,[2] as we knew them, two Jewish women representing Jewish organizations in the area. He also visited us with two very fit young men in their late twenties or early thirties who were experts in hand-to-hand combat. It was rumoured that they worked for British intelligence. One of these men was later killed by gunfire in the streets of Lyon, and the other narrowly escaped arrest. They came to us for respite from time to time.

One day in August 1943, while walking back from Cazaubon, I was stopped by a man stepping out from a Citroën. He asked me, in French, if I was familiar with a Mr. Glasberg. His accent was German, and there were three other men in the car, so I suspected that they were Gestapo. I paused for a few moments, asked him to repeat the name, and explained that I knew a Mr. Lasben, the owner of the flour mill at the other end of the village. The man thanked me, and they drove off in the direction of the village. Many years later I was told by a journalist who was born and raised in this district and who was writing a wartime history of Cazaubon and Barbotan that the Gestapo had arrived at Mr. Lasben's flour mill and physically assaulted him while interrogating him about his true identity, believing him to be Abbé Glasberg. They must have realized their error quite quickly, and so they went to city hall to check the names on the list of residents of our community.

I hurried to the château to tell Mr. Vermont about my encounter with the Gestapo. The mayor's secretary also called to tell Mr. Vermont that the Gestapo was at city hall, checking the list of residents. The château was evacuated by all except Mr. Vermont. A small num-

---

2 Joseph is referring to two social workers: Nina Gourfinkel, who founded DCA (Direction des centres d'accueil, Main Office for the Shelters) with Abbé Glasberg to provide shelter for Jewish refugees in France; and Ninon Haït from EIF (Éclaireurs Israélites de France, Jewish Scouts of France), which was active in the French Resistance.

ber of people lingered from a safe distance to see what would happen. Some of us tried to convince Mr. Vermont to also leave, but he refused. He believed that his arrest could possibly save the centre and allow it to continue to operate.

Approximately one hour after I met the Gestapo on the road, they arrived at the château. They had indeed found Victor Vermont's name on the city hall list and immediately connected his name with Abbé Glasberg. In fact, for a short time they believed that Victor Vermont was Abbé Glasberg. From a safe distance I observed the Citroën parked about fifty metres down the laneway. One of the men remained in the vehicle as the other three walked toward the château. Then I saw Mr. Vermont leave with the three men, and it seemed to me that he had been roughly questioned. After the war I learned that Mr. Vermont lingered in the prisons of Paris and then was deported to Auschwitz. Abbé Glasberg was smuggled out of France to Switzerland in early 1944, and after the war was involved in helping Jews to immigrate to British Mandate Palestine.

Going Underground

Victor Vermont had united the residents of the château, and after his arrest there was no coherent leadership and the number of residents decreased drastically. It was decided that some of the younger members of the château would move out, and some of us were placed on local farms. The mayor of Cazaubon owned a bungalow just outside the village of Barbotan. He made his home, which was hidden from the highway, available for twelve to fifteen older residents of the château.

I was sent north to a village called Saint-Pardoux-la-Rivière to work in a sawmill. It was extremely hard work during a very cold winter, and I was terribly lonely. I had false papers and was trained to answer all possible questions from French gendarmes or Germans, but I made no friends because I feared discovery. I would come home from work to a cold and dark room located at the edge of the village. When I made a fire to heat the room, it often made it smoky so I had to open a window, which would just chill the room again. The nights were extremely cold because it was dangerous to keep the fire burning. It was a very difficult and miserable time for me, and the only respite I had were my visits to Alfred and Lilian in Périgueux, a town close to me. They became like my big brother and sister, and my anchor to civilization.

Alfred and Lilian produced and supplied false papers in the area and also found accommodations for refugees like me who could not find accommodations for themselves. On New Year's Eve of 1943 they organized a party for some of the previous residents of the château at one of the best hotels in Périgueux. We each contributed to the cost of the party and the rooms we stayed in, but Alfred and Lilian helped. The hotel was full of Nazis and SS officers, and we daringly celebrated the new year in their midst! The Germans showed no interest in us, likely believing that their enemies would not dare mingle among them. It was strange celebrating beside our accursed and deadliest of enemies. It was a triumph of sorts, and the party was a much-needed morale boost for all of us. There were rumours the day after that some Germans were killed by their own people. Probably drunkenness and paranoia played a part in the happy tragedy.

The next morning, I returned to the train station to catch the train back to my village and my work at the sawmill. At the station I was caught in a trap of German *Feldgendarmerie* and Gestapo and was arrested. My identity papers were checked and rechecked and passed from one interrogator to the next, each repeating the same questions over again: What was my mother's name, my father's name; what was I doing in this region, since my papers stated I was born in the north; what was I doing in Périgueux; where was I working, and so on. I clearly heard one German telling the other, "Das ist ein ganz verdächtiger bursche" (This is a most suspicious young man), and with this pronouncement they put me against the wall, searched me for weapons and then left me with some other people they believed were suspicious. Others were released after a routine check of their identity papers. I must have played the dimwit convincingly enough, and after some time, they questioned me again and then released me, and I was able to board a later train back to my village.

About two weeks later, I arrived at work one morning and was surprised to find that our power supply and some important machines had been blown up the night before. The sawmill produced barracks for the German army, and the rumour was that those barracks were sent to the Soviet front. The French did not like the idea of their wood and resources being used by the Germans. We were told that we could receive our final payment or wait for further instructions, with the possibility of transferring to another sawmill owned by the same company. I elected to receive my payment and leave, as I had never felt comfortable with the job.

By this time Alfred had moved to Limoges, a city northeast of where I was staying, and was actively involved in the underground resistance, which just barely provided him with an income. I joined him and Lilian, who was assigned to look after me, as she spoke with less of an accent and had a far greater education than I did, even though she was only one year older. She found me work in a ladies' handbag factory, which I had some experience in. I made barely enough money to pay for my rent in a very low-class room-and-board hotel. My room was small, and at night the insects crawled all over the place, including in my bed, which made it difficult to sleep. The food was awful and in short supply because of the war. If you had money, which I did not, the black market was the only place where fresh food could be purchased. From time to time Alfred gave me some extra money or invited me to eat a meal with them or to accompany him to one of his meetings.

It was seen as a great advantage to have our false documents registered and stamped with real city hall stamps. So days after my arrival in Limoges, I went to city hall to register my documents. The clerk looked at me, accused me of having false papers and left with the papers in his hands. I stood at the counter, shocked. Then the clerk returned with my papers stamped, whispered to me with confidence that the papers were false but handed them back to me anyway.

I do not remember the reason I changed jobs, but one day, still in the very early months of 1944, I started to work at a shoe factory. The factory had a contract to repair and restore boots for the German army. My job involved placing steel plates on the front and back of the repaired boots, as well as reinforcing the soles with special nails. There were eight to ten of us doing this job. The factory was very well equipped and had all the then-modern equipment for shoe production. Two or three Germans came to check on us every morning, one of them an *Oberfeldwebel*, senior sergeant. A Jewish shoemaker was assigned to hand-make the boots for the German officers. He feared for his life and was extremely servile to the Germans, which was not to my liking. No one knew that I understood German, and I was afraid to communicate with the Jewish shoemaker in German. Instead, I routinely placed long nails under the plates and under the short nails. One day, during his routine check, the *Oberfeldwebel* discovered several of the boots that I had sabotaged. He started screaming that the boots were tampered with and threatened to have us all shot. No one knew that I was the culprit. The workers all turned white with fear, but the *Oberfeldwebel* didn't follow through on his threat.

On several occasions another worker and I were assigned to travel with the *Oberfeldwebel* in his horse-drawn buggy to deliver boots to the freight trains at the railway station. The German left us to do the job and went to the closest bistro to have some beer. The boots were tied in matching pairs, and during the German's absence we decided to switch the boots to make wildly unfitting matches. We enjoyed this game so much that we completely forgot the danger that was involved. We were never discovered. However, on one occasion as we travelled to the railway station with the officers, I overheard the *Oberfeldwebel* cursing the Jewish shoemaker and swearing that he would send the Jew to his just fate.

Without Alfred's knowledge or consent, I joined the Union de la jeunesse juive, an underground Jewish youth organization affiliated with the movement Main-d'oeuvre immigrée, Immigrant Workers' Union, which was itself affiliated with the French Communist Party. We distributed anti-German literature and tore German propaganda off the walls or changed it by deleting or adding words to contradict the intended meaning. My involvement in these assignments brought me both uneasiness and satisfaction. Later I was involved in helping to transport and hide arms. The Union de la jeunesse juive was organized into cells, each of which had three to four members. Only one member of a cell was connected with another cell. This meant that any one individual in the organization knew the whereabouts of only five to six people at most. This structure was meant to protect the members of the group in case of arrests or betrayals.

One evening after curfew I was assigned to put up and distribute flyers under doorways with another member of my cell. We were caught off-guard by the sound of German boots approaching us. We attempted to seek shelter through several doorways, but every door that we tried was locked. Suddenly one of the doors was unlocked from the inside, and a stranger let us into the entrance of the building and locked the door behind us. The Germans passed us. We eventually returned home, our hearts pounding.

On another evening, as I sat at a long table in the restaurant of our hotel, a group of German *Feldgendarmes* entered the room and sat at the same table as me. They ordered beer and slowly became louder and more boisterous as they began to tell one joke after another. Initially I was able to restrain myself from laughing at their jokes, but suddenly I broke out in laughter. The sergeant sitting across from me looked at me and asked, "Sie verstehen Deutsch?" (You understand German?) Feeling ill at ease, I shook my head. The sergeant continued, in his very limited French, to inquire why I'd laughed. I answered that I had observed the gestures of the soldier telling the joke and found them amusing. He then started a friendly conversation, asking me where I lived and worked. He took the book I was reading and looked at it, turning some of the pages, and then left me alone.

Throughout the war, the Allied forces bombed Gnome et Rhône, a major manufacturer of airplane engines on the outskirts of Limoges. The bombings were frequent and always at night. One morning after one of those bombings, I stepped out of my hotel and noticed two members of my cell in a group of prisoners guarded by German soldiers. The prisoners were clearing the rubble and unexploded bombs at the bombing sites. At the sight of my colleagues, I became weak in the knees but had to walk on as if nothing was wrong. My friends also noticed me but did not betray our connection.

Disaster nearly befell me on another occasion when I was scheduled to meet the leader of our cell. Meetings were scheduled in areas where there were large crowds of people, such as railway stations, city hall, markets and festivals. The time and the day of the meeting was provided with the instruction that if the planned meeting did not occur, it would be attempted at the same time and place the following day. My cell leader was not there at the scheduled time and place, so I tried again the following day. I approached city hall from the other side of the street. I was very happy to see him, but as I was getting ready to extend my hand to greet him, he turned his back to me. At that moment, I noticed a civil guard on each side of him, and I felt my knees once again go weak. I walked between him and one of the civil guards and quickly distanced myself from the trio. The leader later succeeded in escaping from jail, which was next to city hall. His sister found me in my hotel and asked me to help her to get false papers for him so that he could leave Limoges. I was suspicious that it was a trap but agreed to go with her to meet him on the outskirts of the city. When I met with him he explained that the two men he was with at city hall were Gestapo officers who would take him out for long walks and try to ensnare other members of the organization, but thanks to his surreptitious signals to his fellow members, the Gestapo did not succeed. I contacted the people who could take care of his requests, and I know that he was looked after in the end.

As anticipation of the *Débarquement*, the landing in Normandy, grew, I continued working for the organization, distributing propaganda and transporting and hiding arms. Alfred and Lilian continued their work. I remember stealing some stamped documents from the shoe factory so that Alfred could copy them.

One day I entered a coffee shop with Alfred and Lilian. The

waitress approached us and said that a gentleman had been there earlier asking for a Mr. Pell (I am not certain of the name, as Alfred and Lilian changed their names frequently to escape detection and arrest). We ordered coffee so as not to be too obvious, drank it in a hurry and left the coffee shop.

At work people were surprisingly friendly to me. Perhaps my irregular attendance at work caused them to suspect that I was involved in the underground and prompted their enthusiastic warmth, but it made me uncomfortable and added to my mistrust. Two women, one middle-aged and one in her late twenties, offered to do my laundry free of charge. I was also invited to have a modest supper at the older woman's home. Both lived in small, cramped, cheap quarters. Later, when I left Limoges, I left my suitcase containing my meagre belongings with one of the women.

In my position there were ongoing threats and narrow escapes. Late after curfew one night, I heard the sound of heavy German boots nearing my hotel. I looked out the window and saw a patrol of ten Germans marching. They stopped at our hotel. Two stayed behind at the entrance, and the remainder entered the hotel for a search of some sort. I did not know what to do. Was it a routine check? Were they looking for me? Should I try to escape? I was confused. It took time for them to reach the rooms at the top of the building, where I was located. I stretched out on the bed. When they knocked on the door, I pretended to awaken from a deep sleep and asked who it was and what they wanted. The Germans yelled at me to open the door. As I did, I pretended to be drunk with sleep. I handed over my papers and leaned against the wall to prevent my arms and hands from shaking. All went well. They examined my papers and left my room. There were no arrests at the hotel that night. Had they searched my room they would have discovered plenty of incriminating material, including a handgun.

Our organizational cells were constantly shrinking due to frequent arrests. According to my calculations, out of a total of about twenty-one boys, only about four or five of us remained. One morning, as I was having my usual coffee and roll in the kitchen of the hotel, a fascist militiaman approached me. He told me who he was and advised me not to leave the hotel that day. I was completely bewildered. My mind raced as I considered whether or not he was deceiving me — what were his motivations? Was he stating the truth? I calmly responded that I didn't see any reason why I should not leave the hotel. I did leave and walked about sixty to eighty metres when I was stopped and directed to go to a certain spot. The people assembled there were then taken in groups to a movie theatre nearby. We stood in line to be interrogated by a member of the French fascist militia. There were Jews in front of me in the line. Some were afraid to make use of their false papers or could not withstand the questioning, and when they were recognized as Jews, the beatings started without delay. The fascist thugs were relentless with their fists and boots. The louder the screams of protest, the more frenzied and monstrously violent they became.

It was my turn. The questioning went along in a quiet manner, though they insisted that I must have a Jewish parent or grandparent. My steadfast denial and insistence on the identity in my documents gave them some doubts, and they took me to a well-guarded bus with several others. I was taken to a jail where I was placed in a small cell. It was well into the evening when a priest was placed in my cell too. The priest immediately befriended me and started to curse the fascists. He also had some food with him and he offered me some; since I was very hungry, I accepted. We sat there together while he incessantly cursed the fascists. I smelled a provocation, so I interjected, defending them with the justification that they were only doing their job. He slept in the same cell as me that night, and in the morning he was removed. Once again I was questioned, but this time on the subject of anti-Vichy and anti-German activities. I applied my well-practised character of stupidity, and they feigned interest in my opinions on this topic. I had to sleep one more night in the solitude of the cell but was steadfast not to slip out of character.

In the late morning I was taken out of the cell again, this time by a French pro-fascist gendarme. He was much more professional and experienced in the art of interrogation than the amateur militiamen. However, I had the distinct feeling that he had no interest in discovering anything or pushing limits as long as his subject could hold his ground. After about one hour of questioning, the gendarme decided that it was a mistake to keep me any longer. He looked for my documents in the heap on his desk and signed the papers for my release. Those papers had to be signed by three more militiamen, so it took another hour of waiting and again answering the same questions.

By the time I was released, I was hungry but decided that satisfying my hunger would need to wait. I still suspected the possibility of a trap, so I stayed on the streetcars and buses for two hours to ensure that no one was following me. At last I went to Alfred and Lilian's, where I could sit down and eat. They had been worried about me, not knowing my whereabouts. After the incident in the coffee shop, Alfred and Lilian had changed their identities again and gone to live and work in Châteauroux, in central France. I learned later that after the liberation of Châteauroux from the Germans, the liberators found various pictures of Alfred with his many identities in the offices of the Gestapo.

During my time with the underground, communication was difficult since few of us had permanent addresses. One way we communicated was by placing coded ads in local newspapers. For example, "We need blankets and are willing to buy" meant that false identity papers were needed. Another method was using the post office and marking letters *poste restante*, general delivery, meaning that mail could be kept at the post office until picked up. Letters sent this way still had to be written in some form of code.

From late 1943 through early 1944, we had watched with cautious optimism the slow but steady retreat of the German armies. Reading German reports of their retreat from previously held positions gave us hope and a sense of resilience. Individual German soldiers were unable to move around France as freely as they had, so they formed convoys to get around. During this time a fierce propaganda war was being waged for the minds and hearts of the French people. The Germans attempted to convince the population that their so-called saviours and patriots were nothing but worthless foreigners, communists and Jews — in essence, criminals and destroyers of France. I recall one of the more popular German propaganda posters: It had four or five life-sized caricatures negatively depicting foreigners, each one with a non-French name beneath it. The poster claimed that each of these characters was responsible for the deaths of many French people. The sarcastic caption on the poster was "These Are Your Liberators." Our underground and the Allies countered these posters with our own propaganda.

I had become extremely tired and afraid of staying in Limoges, as people there were suspicious of my activities, and many of my comrades had already been arrested. I therefore demanded to meet with the chief commander of all of the units; unfortunately this demand was not so easily granted. Finally, my fervent and incessant requests got me a date and place for a meeting. When the time came, I met a man in his fifties on a busy street. At first he refused to let me leave Limoges. He said that I was needed in the city and not, as I had requested, in a forest unit of the *Maquis*, a resistance group. After I steadfastly refused to remain in Limoges, the man relented and provided me with a tiny piece of paper with an address and code name on it. Before setting out for Argenton-sur-Creuse (Argenton), which was north of Limoges and south of Châteauroux in a forested area, I went to my workplace to pick up my last wages and said goodbye to the foreman and to the two women who had been so concerned about my well-being. They all wished me well.

Resistance

It must have been the end of March 1944 when I boarded the train for Argenton. When I arrived there, I was greeted by a platform full of German soldiers and *Feldgendarmes*. Not wanting to be arrested again, I looked around quickly and decided to approach a railway worker. I told him that I had travelled without a railway ticket. He suggested that I stay put and follow him at a distance once he had finished his task so that he could show me how to leave the station safely. Soon he led me alongside a wooden fence for about a 150 metres, then, with a slight move of his right hand, he indicated a spot on the fence. When I approached the spot, I discovered a loose plank, and I squeezed through the fence. Unfortunately, immediately after I squeezed through the opening, a French gendarme appeared. As was routine, he demanded my identity papers. I was unsure if he'd noticed me sneaking through the fence. Luckily he did not ask too many questions and let me go.

Argenton was approximately six kilometres away from the address I was given, which was in the village of Pont-Chrétien-Chabenet (Chabenet). I was driven directly to the address in Chabenet by a French farmer. It seemed to me, and was later confirmed, that the entire village of Chabenet was involved in anti-German affairs. The farmer was active in the French Communist Party and was the commander of the resistance unit in Argenton; in fact, he controlled the entire area both politically and militarily. It would soon become clear to me that it was dangerous for any French citizen in the area to think of betrayal or collaboration with the Germans, as the consequences were often fatally dealt with by death squads or by a kangaroo court, an impromptu court that often rendered unjust verdicts.

Once I reached the address in Chabenet, I entered a room where some people were relaxing. After checking the tiny piece of paper that the man in Limoges had given me, a man referred to as Commandant Paul spoke with me briefly and then told one of his men to escort me to the encampment, which was not far from the village on the border of the forest. It was composed of several tents made out of parachute material. Part of the Francs-Tireurs et Partisans (Partisan Irregular Riflemen), my unit was called FTP Company 2202. I estimated that the members of the unit were on average just under thirty years old. They were divided into three groups, with one person in command of each group.

The command tent was placed in the centre of the camp. I remember that every afternoon all of us, except those who were on guard duty, would sit around the command tent for at least an hour and a half listening to BBC radio. The purpose behind this daily custom was to listen to coded orders provided to the underground members throughout Europe. Only a few members of the camp understood the coded messages, which included very obtuse phrases, such as "the door will open the wrong way," "the car's tire did explode" and "Mary will celebrate her birthday soon" — all nonsense to those who did not understand the code's translation. Nevertheless, we were fascinated by these messages and knew that some of them might affect us.

On my first day at the camp, I was assigned a semi-automatic rifle with about fifteen rounds of ammunition in the magazine. I was told that the effective firing range was four hundred metres and that the rifle was normally used by commandos and paratroopers. The rifle was light and easy to handle. We also had some Tommy guns and Sten guns, as well as American and British submachine guns to use between us. The most important arms were the Bren fully automatic light machine guns. We also had Mills anti-personnel hand grenades. I was provided with two of these and with one grenade that was very different from anything I had seen before. It was just a pouch filled with plastic explosives, with elastic sewn into the perimeter, a detonator cap and a three-second delay mechanism. I was also provided with clothing that resembled a uniform of sorts. The pants and jackets were French, issued to Vichy paramilitary units; the sweater, boots and socks were from the British army.

On my second night at the camp I was told to join a small unit of six, and we were assigned to march about ten kilometres to detonate the rails on a railway track. There was no training provided. I even had to figure out how to fire my rifle on my own. Once we arrived at the designated location, we checked for the presence of a guard. Most of the time the French guards disappeared before we took control of an area. They didn't want any trouble for their meagre pay and had no desire to put themselves in danger. The destruction of the rail tracks was well organized. Two members of our team walked ahead at a fast pace, two set down the explosives and two guarded from the sides and behind. The explosives were placed at the joints of two rails in order to destroy two rail lines at the same time. There were four joints, and the fuses were set for the time it took to get to the next joint. As the explosives went off, the next load was set and readied, until the job was completed. We took refuge in the forest before our return to the campsite. It usually took the Germans up to two days to repair the damage. But there were so many incidences of sabotage, including of small bridges and water-pumping stations for steam engines, that transportation became very complicated for the Germans, and they often had their hands full with repairs.

Every night, our unit was assigned a different location, and we often had to walk long distances in order to complete our tasks. During the day I also had to do guard duty on a hill overlooking the approach to our encampment. There was one two-week period when we had to endure continuous rain. Our tents weren't waterproof and our entire encampment was drenched. Everything, including our clothing and food, was soaked, yet we had to continue with our activities and nightly treks to target various railway lines and roads. It was demoralizing and physically draining. When the rains subsided and the sun returned, all of our belongings were laid out to dry.

By the end of May 1944, in anticipation of an Allied invasion, the underground had become more courageous and more of a menace to the Germans. We accelerated the destruction of bridges and the obstruction of roads. I especially took pleasure in blocking forest roads by using explosives to down trees over a stretch of one or two hundred metres, which made it impossible for the German tanks to simply push them out of the way. The German soldiers then had to do the back-breaking work of chopping the tree trunks by hand until they could be pushed away by their tanks. Sometimes it would take them nearly two days to clear the road. We were also assigned to ambush German convoys that had fewer than three vehicles. One man from our unit would go ahead to get a clear view of the road and give a signal at the right moment.

One morning, such a moment occurred. We started aggressively firing and throwing grenades at the approaching German convoy. The Germans were surprised by the ambush and in complete disarray; they suffered many casualties. Twelve German prisoners were taken and brought back to our encampment. They were from an air force communications unit and had a truck with very sophisticated equipment.

Several German-speaking members of my unit tried to act as translators during the interrogations of these soldiers, but none were able to do the job well. At one point I was assigned to be the translator for the interrogations and to translate documents, and I was able to do this job to the unit leader's satisfaction, translating quickly and accurately. Eventually I regularly assisted with the interrogation of German prisoners and with the translation of German documents.

Nearly all of the German prisoners asked me where I had learned to speak German so fluently. Initially my answer was that I had learned German because I studied journalism. They mostly doubted this answer but were too intimidated to inquire further. As time passed, I admitted to these prisoners that I was a German-born Jew. This revelation provoked anxiety and humiliation in them, and they would sometimes declare that their parents were staunchly anti-Nazi and that their families did not like Hitler. These vacuous statements did nothing but enrage me.

One very quiet and stoic German soldier in his thirties who was wounded by grenade shrapnel and was obviously suffering from a lack of proper care to his wounds challenged my declaration that Germany was destroyed. He stated that the home front would hold together and that Germany would not collapse like it did in 1918. Both amused and enraged by his ignorance, I immediately provided him with a lesson in simple math: tens of millions of American, Russian and British soldiers; as well as French, Polish, South African, Canadian and Indian troops; and hundreds of thousands in underground movements like ours — versus twenty million German soldiers. I will always remember his answer as he realized the hopelessness of the numbers: "Ja, die sind doch zu viele" (Yes, they are too many). I left him and his hopes completely shattered.

My status in the ranks increased as I became a sought-after translator. I was often in the company of young communist leaders who attempted to influence my thinking. They were an educated group of young men and real idealists who believed that they could change the world for the better. Given my close proximity and relationship to these leaders, I was somewhat influenced by their ideas, but I felt very uncomfortable with their philosophy that the end justified the means. I had been profoundly influenced by the writings of Victor Hugo, Romain Rolland, Panait Istrati, Henri Barbusse, Émile Zola and other humanistic French writers. Nevertheless, we enjoyed each other's company and our discussions about politics. But most of the members of our unit were farmhands and labourers and not formally educated or well-read. One of the rank-and-file members bragged that he could not be categorized as an uneducated farmer since he had regularly visited the nearest town of twenty thousand people.

Our activities in the days leading to and immediately after the Allied invasion of Normandy on June 6, 1944, became more intense and strenuous. We were all suffering from extreme exhaustion. I often found myself sleepwalking. Whenever we stopped to rest, everyone collapsed into slumber. The assigned guards were unable to stay alert for more than ten or fifteen minutes at a time, and so we had to establish a rotation on an honour basis, where the guard on duty would wake up the person next in line as soon as he was unable to guard any longer.

Our ranks increased as it became clear that the tide of the war was turning, and the people decided to take up arms rather than submit to the Germans. But we learned that the Germans were conducting brutal reprisals, killing hostages in revenge for the guerilla attacks. In one infamous reprisal, in Tulle, on June 9, 1944, after arresting all the men between the ages of sixteen and sixty, the 2nd SS Panzer Division *Das Reich* and members of the SD, the intelligence service of the SS, hanged ninety-nine of the prisoners and sent 149 to the Dachau concentration camp, where 101 of them were murdered.

The most tragic and brutal massacre occurred in Oradour-sur-Glane on June 10, 1944. The *Das Reich* SS division involved in the Tulle massacre, led by SS-*Hauptsturmführer* Adolf Diekmann, surrounded the village. They ordered all the villagers — and anyone who happened to be in or near the town — to gather in the village square, allegedly to have their identity papers checked. They later claimed to be searching for arms, and used this as a pretext for separating the women and children — who were locked in the church while the village was searched — from the men, who were taken to six barns and shot. The soldiers then set the barns on fire. Only six men escaped; one of them was later shot dead. The soldiers set fire to the church and shot those who tried to escape. In a matter of hours, 642 inhabitants of Oradour-sur-Glane and the surrounding villages were murdered. Adolf Diekmann claimed that the episode was a retaliation for partisan activity in nearby Tulle and the kidnapping of *Sturmbannführer* Helmut Kämpfe by the French Resistance the day before.

After this we coordinated with other guerilla forces to change our campsite frequently. We often used the ruins of old châteaux as encampments. One day we were ordered to quickly vacate a château on a hill. As we arrived at the edge of the forest about one and a half kilometres from the château, we saw about two hundred Germans in trucks and motorcycles arrive. We watched them prepare light artillery in the fields at the base of the hill and then storm the hill from all sides. They must have been disappointed to find the château vacated, and it was most entertaining for us to witness their disappointment.

The steady growth in our numbers caused logistical problems. We didn't have sufficient food supplies, which meant that there was excessive rationing. We had to be constantly on the move, and that was not easy with all of our equipment and ammunition. We had some trucks and Citroën automobiles, which were the preferred vehicles for the police, Gestapo and underground for their speed and ability to cross rough terrain. The underground usually confiscated Citroëns from people they often justifiably believed to be collaborators. But the vehicles had to be loaded and unloaded quickly, and our encampments had to be assembled and disassembled often. The leadership also became less effective, and there was no individual or unit training. Two French army reserve officers presented themselves to the guerilla units after General Charles de Gaulle, the leader of the Free French Forces in Britain, appealed to the French to continue fighting in June 1944; they were assigned to train us, but they lacked the necessary skills and enthusiasm.

The whole command structure was inadequate, and officers from the Army of Africa, which had united with de Gaulle's Free French Forces, were recruited to improve it. One of these officers was in our encampment. Initially, I was impressed by his appearance and his ability to establish some order in our unit, which had now reached over a hundred members. However, fifty more members arrived from an independent Spanish unit consisting of people with past activities in the Spanish Civil War. As the Spaniards arrived and our numbers swelled, I lost the respect I'd had for our new commander. He was not as brave and courageous as some of the less trained commanders. It turned out that the leaders of our unit were mostly members of the Communist Party.

The disorderliness in our division led to indiscriminate executions and death sentences of collaborators and traitors, and the lack of discipline led to chaos and unauthorized implementation of procedures. Those responsible for the administration of justice played God, completely disregarding not only laws and orders but basic morality. The command eventually eliminated these members.

Within our group there was one young man born in Alsace-Lorraine, which had been part of Germany before World War I. Historically, this area had always been disputed and changed hands during many wars. He was of course fluent in French and German. One day the commanding officer of our unit came looking for him. When he was nowhere to be found, the officer panicked and organized an urgent search for him. He was later found hiding on a farm and was accused of espionage and treason. I witnessed the trial and was not satisfied with the proceedings of the kangaroo court. I wasn't convinced there was sufficient proof of his guilt. Nevertheless, he was sentenced to be executed. A priest was brought in to give him his last rites, and he was then executed by a firing squad of ten men, two of whom did not have live ammunition in their rifles — a way to diffuse a sense of responsibility among the men for killing one of their own. Less than one day had passed between his disappearance, trial and execution.

After his execution, I thought back to his behaviour. He had guarded the German prisoners with sadistic brutality, often kicking them or pouring water over the shackled prisoners in the middle of the night and leaving them to shiver in the cold. He was also fond of making antisemitic comments, which I ascribed to his exposure to German and fascist propaganda. He occupied my thoughts for some time. My feelings were muddled with disdain for his brutal behaviour and remorse for his untimely and unjust demise.

At one point our camp commander received an oral command to kill all the German prisoners. He demanded that this order be made in writing. A written order was forwarded to him on the margin of a small piece of newspaper. The camp commander then ordered all members of our group to appear for roll call and explained that he had a dilemma. Showing us the written order on the piece of news-print, he explained that according to the Geneva Conventions he could not simply kill the German prisoners and that the written or-der on the bit of newsprint was not sufficient for him to contravene the Conventions. He said that if anyone in the group was willing to carry out the order and take responsibility for his actions, he may go ahead and do so, but as far as he was concerned he would not execute the order. There were arguments and discussions within our ranks for many days after that. In the end no one dared take responsibility for the execution of the Germans.

~

I once had the opportunity to participate in a parachute drop of arms and provisions. A number of us assembled at dusk, and I was as-signed to travel to the drop site in a large truck, while others travelled in smaller trucks and Citroëns. Arriving at a clearing surrounded by forest vegetation, we were met by about twenty-five members of the AS, Armée secrète, the wing of the *Maquis* that was loyal to General de Gaulle and was now part of the Forces Françaises de l'Intérieur, French Forces of the Interior (FFI). Our leaders met with their lead-ers, and an animated discussion ensued regarding which group was to be the rightful receiver of the parachute drop. The other group left, only because they were hopelessly outnumbered by our group. The struggle for political power among the various *Maquis* groups was constant, and access to arms was at its forefront. No member of one group dared to enter the territory of another with weapons, as it was certain that they would be disarmed.

As darkness descended, we positioned ourselves around the clearing to ready ourselves for the parachute drop and secure our surroundings from any further interference. After about two hours we heard the engines of an airplane flying relatively low overhead. Light signals were activated in the clearing and on the perimeter of the field, and the plane flew into sight, circled us once and then discharged its load, raining down cylindrical containers attached to parachutes. They came down much faster than anticipated, and the collection of the containers started immediately. We had to pay attention so as not to be rapped on the head by another falling container. The containers were heavy and were designed with four handles so that they could be quickly removed from the field by four people. Some of the containers were difficult to open as they had been dented in the drop, but generally speaking the valuable goods were delivered in good condition. The contents included arms, ammunition and plastic explosives, all of which were cushioned at the bottom of the container by military clothing, boots, pullovers and socks. Everyone participated, removing the containers from the field as quickly as possible. They were brought to waiting trucks, which sped away with their escort vehicles once they were fully loaded. The trucks travelled at top speed on the unpaved forest path under low-hanging tree branches. The drivers were all locals and were familiar with every turn on the path. Each truck was brought to a different hidden location to be unloaded.

One of our large assignments after the Allied invasion was to blow up and destroy the viaduct in Chabenet. The bridge carried the railway line used for transportation between Paris and Toulouse. It stretched over a deep, wide valley and was very high, long and narrow. The Allied air force had tried to bomb it several times, but the bombs had just fallen harmlessly into the valley. We were rarely all assigned to one activity together, but one evening, our entire encampment assembled for the assignment. When we arrived at the appointed location, we were met by more people, and we assumed positions from which we could guard the operation. We were told that over five hundred kilograms of plastic explosives were planted on the bridge. Word came for us to move to safety, and as we crossed the bridge we could see the explosives strategically placed between two pillars. We moved to very high ground on the mountain just over the tunnel that the railway line went through. When the blast took place, we were thrown to the ground; the explosion reverberated through the valley and there was a change in the air pressure. We covered our heads and ears as we heard small rocks falling from above us, but no one was hurt. The railway line was put back into service only after the liberation of the area from the Germans.

Around this time I had two narrow escapes. First, I made an error in my translation of a document during the interrogation of a German non-commissioned officer (NCO). The German had denied the allegations in the document and pointed out to me that I had misread one sentence. I admitted this to the questioning officer, but he was not entirely convinced that it was an innocent error. He told me bluntly that if it was an honest mistake nothing would happen, but if I was trying to cover up or assist the prisoner, then I was in big trouble. I insisted that it was a mistake. Two other men were brought in to review the document, and to my great relief they confirmed that it was an innocent mistake.

The second occurrence was the discovery by my comrades that I was secretly writing a daily journal, which I knew they disapproved of. There was some mistrust between the French-born non-Jewish members of my group and me, and one of these members tore the journal away from me while I was writing. They were puzzled by what I wrote and started screaming loudly that I was a traitor. My journal was brought to the command tent, and I was put under guard. After what seemed like a long time, the second-in-command, who was a young communist, called me to his tent. He spoke to me in a polite and enlightened fashion. He started by commenting that having an opinion was acceptable, even if it was different from his. Then he asked me pointedly, "What if your diary fell into the hands of the Germans?" Of course, I had no answer to this legitimate question. My journal was a record of all my activities and my thoughts and analyses of circumstances as they arose. My words were sometimes critical of the command and the organization, which was why I was afraid of it being discovered. This officer's gentle, civilized and sympathetic reaction to the contents of my journal surprised me. In retrospect I believe that it was indicative of a broad education and tolerance of diversity. My journal was kept by the officer.

One evening a Citroën arrived at the encampment, stirring our curiosity. We all approached the car slowly. The driver, in the uniform of a lieutenant, stepped out of the vehicle. I immediately recognized him as a colleague from my time in Limoges, so I called out to him loudly, "Léon!" Another member in my group asked abruptly, "Another Jew?" and turned toward the lieutenant with his hand on his holster. The immediate interference by another officer prevented the situation from escalating. This incident highlighted to me the unfortunate prevalence of antisemitism in the underground.

Antisemitism was not unknown in the rest of France either. I once attended a meeting in a village controlled by the AS with two other men. As a favour to a colleague in our encampment, I was to find a friend of his in the village. Once our meeting with the captain of the village command ended, I asked the captain if he knew where I could find this person. The captain abruptly asked if I was Polish. I said no, and he asked why I wished to see this man. I answered that I was Jewish and that I had been informed that this man was Jewish too. The captain responded, "We French do not like the Jews either, but we are not as barbaric as the Germans. My counsel to you is that you should not interfere in our problems and that you should stay out of it." The captain was not thrilled to see me with members of the FTP. Back at the camp, the two colleagues with whom I had attended the meeting recounted the story to our command. I was called to the command tent to confirm the episode with our captain. The two officers of our camp were incensed by the captain's conduct and wanted to pursue some form of reprisal. I was uninterested in taking action and dissuaded them from doing so. By this stage I had made up my mind that I was going to immigrate to British Mandate Palestine after the war.

~

By early July 1944, in the forests south of Châteauroux, the membership of the underground must have reached around five hundred fighters. From the cover of these forests, the underground planned and instigated numerous attacks and ambushes against the Germans. At this time, the Germans were desperate to move north to help their troops there resist the Allied attacks, but the progress of the German units was severely hindered by the rampant destruction of their transportation methods. The roads and the railway system were targeted repeatedly, and the German units were constantly ambushed and attacked on the roads and from the air. The Germans started to show signs of disintegration and collapse, with small groups of soldiers that were separated from their units becoming easy prey. Deserters who were lost and wandering through the forest also began to appear. Some of the bigger units started to use horses and wagons for transportation because their gasoline had run out. The well-oiled German army machine was showing signs of breaking down, which made it an easier target for us. However, some larger German units still remained, and these continued to present a challenge to the underground because of their superior training, strategic knowledge, combat discipline and command capabilities. Our actions against these larger German units were limited to hit-and-run operations that were carried out on an intense and frequent scale.

There was an unfortunate consequence of our successful attempts to immobilize the Germans: the whole forested area of Châteauroux was eventually surrounded by them. Since nearly all transportation routes were severed, our enemies were in close proximity, competing with us for scarce resources. Both our units and those of the Germans had to plunder the neighbouring farms for food. Our units did leave receipts with the farmers for the future government to honour, but many farmers still fled the area. We were all suffering from extreme hunger, and whenever possible we would forage for wild berries.

Eventually, we found an abandoned pig farm. All that remained on this farm were a few swine. One of these was immediately slaughtered and cooked in water with no salt or seasonings. By evening we each received a fairly generous piece of pork with no other food. After downing this meal, my stomach violently revolted, and all that night I surrendered what I believed to be my soul to God.

There were approximately fifteen German prisoners among us who were crammed into what had been pigpens. Some of the German prisoners were deserters, or they had become separated from their units and were lost, or they were from the pro-German Ukrainian army (especially despised by us as traitors of the Soviet Union). These German prisoners were guarded by the Spanish units within our group, and the perimeter of the farm was guarded by our regular units.

One morning I agreed to dress up in a German uniform in order to survey the area and determine what was happening on the road. In retrospect, this was a foolish tactic that could have cost me my life. I went out onto the road with about ten men behind me. I was extremely lucky that no Germans showed up. Relieved, I walked back to the farm with my escorts. A short time after our return to the farm, we were attacked by a German unit. However, we must have had some intelligence about the impending attack as the units guarding the perimeter of the farm had been tripled and armed with machine guns. The Germans deployed in a broad formation, attacking us from different points in the field. They came from many directions on their infamous motorcycles with machine-gun-toting sidecars, firing at us from all sides. We were confused and panicked. I was extremely anxious because I was still wearing the German uniform and was worried that one of my unit members who didn't know about my wanderings in the uniform would confuse me for a German and shoot me in panic. The first thing I did was fling off my jacket and put on a British pullover. I also rid myself of the German rifle and found my own smaller rifle, but I was still wearing the German uniform pants. The fighting with the Germans was short-lived, and remarkably, given their numbers, we suffered only a few casualties. We then retreated into smaller, fragmented and disorganized units.

I remember that before we left the farm, I witnessed the most horrifying of scenes. The Spaniards who had been guarding the German prisoners threw hand grenades into their small and cramped quarters. Some of the prisoners staggered out of the pens all bloodied, only to be gunned down by the guards.

Somehow, we succeeded in returning to our previous forest base, which was close to Chabenet. This time we stayed at an old, neglected château that was close to the village. The German prisoners that we'd left behind there had somehow disappeared.

At the end of the summer, the regional command decided to conquer and occupy Châteauroux. There were only a few *Feldgendarmes* left as they had moved out as soon as they noticed the French moving in. This was a short-lived endeavour, as the Germans decided to return to guard this major centre for communications and transportation routes. So they re-conquered this location without much resistance. About two weeks later the Germans retreated from the area, killing about a dozen citizens from Châteauroux as they left, just to emphasize their control. A large victory parade was organized on September 11, 1944, and on the honour podium stood two American colonels, members of a special unit that coordinated sabotage and hit-and-run operations for the Allied forces.

〜

Shortly after this parade I became very sick with an infectious skin rash. I received some money and medicated cream and was placed in a village hotel to rest and recover. On my first night at the hotel I overheard some people speaking Dutch, which I was familiar with from my time in Belgium. I greeted the group — an older gentleman, a younger woman and a boy who was about twelve years old — by wishing them a good day in Dutch and was immediately invited to their table at the hotel restaurant. The gentleman told me that he had been a judge in Ceylon (now Sri Lanka), a former colony of the Netherlands. He urged me to eat and drink without consideration to the cost. Every time I entered the hotel restaurant he invited me to sit at their table. I didn't know what to make of this situation, as he didn't mention that he was paying for my meals. I feared that the money I had would not be enough to pay for all the food I'd ordered, so I decided to check out early. When I went to the hotel desk to settle my account, I was told that all my expenses had already been taken care of. I was sorry that I had decided to check out so early and was so grateful for this act of kindness shown to me when I was sick and alone.

After that I stayed for a day or two in a hotel room in Châteauroux where I discovered a huge, neatly bundled stack of old German newspapers. I skimmed through the articles and was fascinated by the way the propaganda was woven into every article, news story, column — everything that was written. The newspaper was a coordinated effort to disseminate false information to the German population. I was entranced by my discovery and spent the whole day reading these newspapers. By late afternoon I began to wonder: If I had not been born a Jew, and persecuted because of that, would I also have succumbed to this machinery of propaganda? Would I have been any different than the general German population?

Reunion and Renewal

The liberation of Belgium, which began in September 1944, left me feeling extremely restless. I was anxious to know the whereabouts of my mother and sister, having had no contact with them for over two years. My repeated requests to return to Brussels were refused by my command, and I considered defecting and trying to reach Brussels on my own. However, having witnessed the treatment of other defectors who were caught, I decided against it. The Jewish lieutenant Léon from Limoges visited our camp, and I asked him for help locating my mother and sister in Brussels. He immediately sat down with me to outline a letter that he would give to our commander requesting my participation on a mission with the Belgian army in the final struggle against the Germans. In the meantime, I was included in a lineup of about a dozen men who were on a proposed list to join the *École de cadre*, the school of NCOS, as soon as our units were integrated into the French army. I was proud and flattered to be among the selected men. Yet, despite this honoured recognition, I was resolved to find my mother and sister and immigrate to Palestine.

I told the members of my unit that I was not French, but they challenged that idea. They strongly believed that after fighting together, I was superior to most French citizens. At my insistence, Lieutenant Léon gave his letter to Commandant Paul, who signed with the stipulation that Commander Alex of Châteauroux had the final word on my placement. I was given permission to travel to Châteauroux to meet with Alex. He not only signed the letter but added in his own handwriting that all authorities on my journey to Brussels should give me any form of assistance I required. Commander Alex's additional comment on the letter proved to be most helpful in my passage within a war-ravaged country where travel was restricted. Every official I came across honoured and respected the commander's request. The final permission to leave was provided to me on September 23, 1944.

I bid goodbye to a few close friends, packed my belongings, travelled to Châteauroux and then waited all day for a train to Limoges, where I was going in order to retrieve my belongings. Meandering alone in the city, I discovered photographs of the liberation parade in which I had participated displayed in a photography store window. I went into the store and purchased two of the photographs. I boarded a train to Limoges that evening and arrived by nightfall. I attempted to find a reasonably priced hotel to sleep in with no success. Suddenly I was struck with the idea that I could sleep on the train in one of the sleeping carriages. I went back to the railway station and gave one of the guards a pack of tobacco and a pack of cigarettes in exchange for permission to board one of the carriages.

In the morning, dressed in my uniform, I proudly visited the hotel I had lived in while residing in Limoges. I then visited the shoe factory I had worked at, only to learn that the owner had been arrested for collaboration with the German enemy. The factory was still operational, and the foreman allowed me to walk around freely. I met the two women who had assisted me, and then I retrieved my belongings from the one who was holding them for me. I also took this opportunity to speak with the Jewish shoemaker whom I had reviled for his eager servility to the Germans. I made a point of speaking Yiddish and German, and he seemed to be embarrassed by the discovery that I was also Jewish. The remaining workers were also surprised to hear me speaking fluent German.

The next morning, my travel northward to Belgium started with the train ride back to Châteauroux, this time by daylight. I was now able to see the temporary repairs to the sabotaged viaduct, over which the train had to travel very slowly. The letter I carried stated that I was not required to pay for my train transportation. However, from Châteauroux to Orléans, all the rails were totally destroyed and no train travel was available, as the Allied forces had tried to prevent German reinforcements from arriving at the northern front. My transportation on this leg of my journey involved a Citroën fueled by wood gas, a driver and another passenger in the back. The passenger was the wife of a French general who had been arrested and brought to Paris for trial for his collaboration with the Vichy government. This woman was crying and complaining to me how inconsiderate it was of the French forces to arrest her husband, who was the epitome of a good patriot and loyal servant of France. I really had no sympathy for her, but I said nothing and just wished for a swift arrival in Orléans. Unfortunately, we had to stop frequently to check on the fire in car's oven. As we approached Orléans I saw how devastated this part of the country was. The destroyed rails had formed into grotesquely shaped twisted metal, and the railway cars were just burned-out skeletal remains, piled high like shattered pyramids of scrap metal.

When we reached Orléans I went to the railway station to inquire about transport to Paris. Someone directed me to the station manager who, seeing my letter, wrote out a voucher for a special train that was scheduled to leave shortly after my arrival. While I was boarding, I noticed the general's wife crying and begging to be allowed onto the train. What irony, I thought. Me, the formerly hunted and persecuted, suddenly receiving preferential treatment over the wife of a French general. The train I boarded was assigned to American soldiers, but because my letter stated that I was travelling to join a special mission, the Americans generously invited me to join them. Two American soldiers asked me if I was Jewish. When I answered that I was, they asked if I knew that it was Yom Kippur. I had no idea. Those two Americans remained with me on the journey to Paris and shared their refreshments with me.

We arrived in Paris late at night and I wandered the streets, not really knowing where to go. I had very little money left, but my wandering brought me to the front door of the cheap hotel where I had lodged before my escape to the south. It was two in the morning when I rang the bell; the door was answered by the owner, whom I knew from when I stayed there. He embraced me joyfully and told me how happy he was to discover that I had survived. I was extremely surprised and touched that he recognized me so quickly after more than two years, and to learn that he had known that it was illegal to house me with my false papers. The owner gave me one of his small, cheap rooms. In the morning, when he asked for my papers to register me, I told him that those too were not in my true name. After I told him that I intended to travel that day, he cancelled the registration.

At the railway station I was given a pass to travel northward to Arras. Again, it was a predominantly military train. After some time travelling, the train stopped at a village and everyone disembarked. I went to the nearby highway hoping to catch a ride. An American military convoy saw my uniform and picked me up, and I travelled on this truck until Arras, at which point the convoy headed in a different direction.

By this time it was evening, and I needed to look for somewhere to sleep. Nearly the entire town of Arras had been destroyed. I asked a group of American soldiers if they knew of a place to stay, and after asking me if I minded where I slept, they directed me to a nearby address. When I arrived I was led into a large room with a group of American and British soldiers in the midst of many girls. I soon realized that this was a brothel and felt very uncomfortable. Suddenly a brawl broke out, the British soldiers fighting the American soldiers. Chairs were flying, tables were overturned and the girls ran off screaming. I took this opportunity to leave. Wandering the streets of Arras again, I came across a school building where there was a group of French *Maquis* and some escaped Soviet prisoners of war. They were fully armed and sleeping on the floor of the gym. I presented my papers and was immediately permitted to join them.

In the morning I walked toward the highway searching for transportation northward to Belgium. Luck presented itself in the form of a British sergeant in a Jeep and a British soldier in a small pickup truck who were heading back to their units. They were friendly and shared the meals that they prepared on a field stove. We arrived at the Belgian border, and I showed my papers and explained to the customs and border guard my history and the reason I wanted to return to Brussels. The guard spoke to his superiors and gave me permission to pass, and I continued to ride with the British sergeant and soldier. I confided to my travel escorts the reason for my journey and the anxiety I felt about my mother and sister. When we arrived in Brussels, the British soldiers refused to leave me and insisted on driving me around until I found my mother. We drove from address to address until suddenly I had the idea of checking with the Spanish smugglers. There the patriarch of the family had one of the young girls show me to my mother's new residence. Only after I was reunited with my mother did the British soldiers finally leave me.

The meeting with my mother was emotional and surprising for both of us. I was very worried about how emaciated she looked. She had always had a plump, round appearance, and now she was shrunken and gaunt-looking. The years of suffering were unmistakably etched into her face and showed in her demeanour. During our first few months together, all the suffering was revealed in story after story. She had had to work for paltry and insufficient food, and for shelter, was shuffled from place to place and treated like a possession. People exploited her for her sewing abilities and treated her like a servant. She'd had to place my sister in a Catholic institution that found her shelter with other families so that she could continue working without worrying about my sister's daily well-being. My mother was stressed constantly, fearing that her presence would be betrayed to the Nazis, and she had incessant angst about my sister. There were, however, moments of humanity. One day upon her return to our old apartment, she was grabbed while walking down the long, dark hall leading to the back of the building. It was the landlord, saving her from being discovered by the Germans, who were at that moment searching the building for any remaining Jews.

After I arrived in Brussels, I became extremely ill for two to three months with one sickness after another. The releasing of tension could have been a factor. The first ailment was the return of the festering skin sores that I had experienced in France. The doctor I saw warned me about the infectiousness of the sores. My mother and sister and I had to go to the local hospital and undergo painful scrubbing in sulphur baths. It was a most distasteful treatment, as the smell of rotten eggs was on our bodies and in our home for several days afterwards. We also had to boil all of our clothes and bedding on a daily basis in order to kill the germs. The next ailment came in the form of many painful boils that disabled me, preventing me from leaving home. Finally, I suffered a bout of bronchitis.

When my health finally stabilized, I was able to look for employment. The first job I found was with a belt manufacturer, which was similar to my previous work with leather goods. However, the glue used in the manufacture of the belts was made from natural rubber and gasoline, and inhaling the fumes all day eventually made me violently ill. I was unable to digest any food and was nauseous, vomiting anything I ate. I had to look for another job and found one with my old employer, a leather goods manufacturer. He had survived the war with his family, hidden in the villages surrounding Brussels by some of his employees. After the liberation he rented a large house and restarted his factory. He was hiring many new employees, as the demand for goods was intense. After so many years of war there was a renewed hunger for merchandise. I quickly became his foreman, but I understood this was only because there was not a more mature and experienced person available. And so, at eighteen years old, I became the foreman of a factory with thirty to forty employees.

The youth of our community started to have active and fruitful social lives. We met almost every evening to read and discuss political issues with a desire to contribute to building a better world. We were a shrewd and perceptive group and were able to foresee, prior to public discussion in the newspapers or on the radio, the future clashes that would occur between the former allies — the United States and the Soviet Union.

In December 1944, the campaign of German General Field Marshal Gerd von Rundstedt, known as the Ardennes Offensive, worried us. A large group of Jewish youth went to the Belgian and United States army offices to volunteer for service. We were turned away and told to go home and not to worry. Shortly after that the offensive was defeated, and the Allied forces marched deep into Germany. The collapse of Germany was imminent, and life was normalizing. The fear of a possible negative turn of events no longer haunted us, but the streets were still full of British and American soldiers. There was also a substantial black market in army clothing and other materials that the soldiers sold for extra cash.

The penetration of the Allied forces into previously held German territories resulted in the emancipation of the concentration camps. Of the survivors who came to Belgium, only a minority had been there prior to the war. The majority of them had never lived in Belgium, and most of them were from Poland. We began to hear about the horrific realities of existence in the camps. We saw people who were completely emaciated, or worse, suffering from bloating caused by starvation. The stories we heard were astonishing, and some of the survivors' behaviour reflected the suffering they had endured. They would laugh hysterically at the sight of people enjoying themselves at the fairgrounds and yell about how absolutely insane this was.

My mother took charge of two young girls my age whom I'd encountered and brought home. They were both from Poland and spoke only Polish, though one of them was able to speak a little Yiddish. These two girls later accompanied us on our journey to Palestine and married in Israel. One of them kept in touch with my mother for many years after our arrival.

Belgium's government-in-exile had returned from the United

Kingdom in September 1944, relatively prosperous because of the Belgian Congo's valuable natural resources, such as rubber. The economy grew due to new economic policies as well, and black-market prices of essential goods went down. By the time the Germans were driven out of Belgium in February 1945, food supplies were more available. So day by day, life normalized, in fact much sooner than it did in France or in the Netherlands, where there had been much more damage to railways, roads and dikes. With every week that passed, more Jews returned to Brussels from the surrounding villages, from France and from all sorts of other hiding places. Yet the social structure of the Jewish community did not revert back to the pre-war or the pre-1942 eras. Now there was no differentiation between Jewish refugees and the older, integrated Jewish inhabitants of Belgium. What remained was one Jewish community, united by their experiences and the suffering brought on by the war. Among the remaining youth, there was a strong desire to immigrate to Palestine. At the beginning of 1945, the Jewish Zionist movement was divided into the traditional political streams. I opposed the split and was sorry to see it happen. I reluctantly decided to join Hashomer Hatzair, a definitively leftist organization.

The socialist party of Belgium opened up the university to workers, and a substantial number of us joined. A former prime minister of Belgium was the director and teacher of political science, history and economics. I attended the university almost every evening until I left Belgium. After waking up at five in the morning, my daily routine included meeting with a group of friends to read together for an hour or two and then going to work. I was envious of the students I saw commuting to high school or university for the day. After work I met with my friends at the university or at the Zionist club for more reading and discussion, or sometimes for a social dance.

My position as a foreman admittedly started to inflate my ego somewhat, and I quit this job in order to start my own business. With the financial help of my business partner's father, we set up our own shop in the small flat I shared with my family, just like many of the small shops in Poland and Belgium before the war. My mother was a big help with our sewing needs. In this small, crowded flat we had fourteen employees. I had no problem selling our products. The market was still so hungry for merchandise that each time I went out to sell, I returned home with enough work to keep us busy for two or three weeks. The first question any potential buyer would ask was, "When are you able to deliver?" The price was only a secondary consideration, and we made a substantial profit on our sales. I later realized that I wasn't prepared for such success, and I didn't understand the value of money, spending it freely and often foolishly. My main weakness was to donate it to any organization that asked, especially Zionist organizations. Donating money made me feel important and welcome.

One of the activities I cherished was the sale and distribution of the Hashomer Hatzair magazine. I also wrote some articles for this magazine with the help of a friend and Belgian Holocaust survivor who assisted me with my spelling.

During late 1944 and early 1945, we were still bombarded by V1 and V2 missiles. Britain and Belgium were the main recipients of those new and devastating missiles. The V1 rocket was less effective, since it was slower and very noisy; in fact, it was more like an unmanned aircraft than a missile, and so it was not difficult to down. People would listen to the noise of the missile and know that when the sound stopped, it would hit shortly, and so they had enough time to seek shelter. Shelters were made available everywhere. The explosives that this missile carried were considerable. The V2 was a much more destructive weapon, as it did not give a noisy warning of its approach. It also had no accuracy, and so it caused indiscriminate damage wherever it fell, especially in populated areas. In Britain, people often slept in shelters because there was no advance warning system. Our anxiety was raised considerably by these missiles.

Early one morning we woke up to a loud noise. We were shaken by the sound of breaking dishes as the kitchen cabinet collapsed and the plaster fell from the crumbling ceiling. All of us ran screaming down the stairs to the inner courtyard of the building, but the danger had passed before we even started running. We could see the devastation caused by the missile when we walked along the streets that same day. With the advance of the Allied forces, these bombings soon diminished, until they finally stopped altogether.

~

On May 8, 1945, Germany formally surrendered. I remember vividly the celebrations in Brussels, especially those at night. People danced everywhere, in the streets and in the squares. The city was crowded with masses of people in happy revelry. I sat with friends on the wall of the Palais de Justice, located high on the hill overlooking the city, watching the city lights as they twinkled for the first time in many years. We talked sadly about the nearly five years of torment and the countless unjust deaths. From there we descended through the narrow streets of the city and strolled from place to place, participating at times, yet also burdened with thoughts of the great cost to humanity and to Jewish lives in particular. The joy was bittersweet and tainted by the anguish and grief of profound loss.

Part II

Am Yisrael Chai

Our lives now had momentum; we were heading toward normalcy. People rushed to work, and merchandise, especially food, became more abundant. But the vision of most of the Jewish community was to immigrate to Palestine. To our surprise, permission was granted for us to leave for Palestine soon after the V-Day celebrations in May 1945. The Zionist organization announced that from the over twenty thousand immigration certificates that had been issued by the British before the war and remained unused, there was an allocation for us in Brussels. Members of Hashomer Hatzair discussed the allocation and decided who would receive the certificates. It was soon made clear that I would get a certificate but that my mother and my sister would not. My business partner's father was on the board of both the Jewish Agency and a Zionist organization in Brussels. He, his son, daughter and son-in-law were also scheduled to depart for Palestine immediately. At my request he sought certificates for my mother and sister, and he succeeded in including them in this wave of aliyah.

We were scheduled to depart several times, but the departures were postponed, which resulted in hardships for some of us. Our first scheduled departure did not leave me with much time to organize our belongings and sell off our inventory. The first department store I approached bought the entire inventory at a discount and paid for it two hours after its delivery. We gave up our apartment and furniture, then because of the postponements, we had to live in a refugee centre for a while. During our stay at the centre, many Jewish soldiers from the British and American armies visited. They were most welcome visitors; we enjoyed their company and they made us feel very proud.

Near the end of the summer, the day finally arrived, and the departure took place in a convoy of trucks from the Jewish Brigade, a unit of Jewish soldiers from Palestine who fought in the British army. On the sleeves of their uniforms there was an insignia similar to the Israeli flag: the Star of David in the middle of a blue and white background. Seeing these Jewish soldiers, we were overcome with positive emotions. For us, their appearance was a declaration that the people of Israel were alive — *Am Yisrael chai, chai v'kayam* (The people of Israel live, live and endure). We boarded the convoy of trucks, arriving in Paris in the late afternoon after a pleasant trip. We were lodged at a good hotel that was reserved for the many refugees of the war who were travelling, and we were given food and all our necessities. Our stay in Paris lasted about five days, allowing me to visit some of my friends from my time in France. One morning we were told that we had to pack, and we were then taken to the railway station to board a train to Marseille. The train was filled not only with our group but with Jews from all over France.

Our trip to Marseille was uneventful but filled with high spirits. In Marseille we were met by a long convoy of American military trucks that transported us to an old military camp in the vicinity of Toulon. Again we had to wait for about one week. More Jews arrived, some joining us from Switzerland. We had no restrictions on our movements, and I took the opportunity to enjoy wandering the streets of Marseille. There were organized activities and tours to the nearby French Riviera. On one occasion we passed a military camp that held German prisoners of war. We spontaneously started to sing, "Am Yisrael chai, chai v'kayam."

Among our growing group of émigrés were a substantial number of young people without the required immigration certificate, and so

according to British Mandate Palestine, they were illegal. The thinking was that we would be able to smuggle them on board our ship. I
argued with the elders of our group that, given the post-war chaos,
now was the perfect time to break the rules. I was right. We were
never checked on our way from Brussels to Paris. The respect for my
opinion was high, as my experience with the underground had given
me a good understanding of the situations we came across.

On the day that we were to board the ship, the American convoy returned to take us to the docks in Toulon harbour, where our
ship was anchored and waiting. There was concern regarding how to
smuggle the illegals onto the ship since the British were organizing
the embarkation. Our opportunity came with the call for volunteers
to carry the many suitcases on board as the names of the certificate
holders were called out. I assigned the illegals the task of carrying the
suitcases. We were provided with pins to place on our jackets, but the
British were understaffed and unable to take our names. We passed
the pins to the illegals and ensured that the pins were returned to us
so that we could then give them to the next wave of illegals to carry
more suitcases onto the ship. The scheme worked, and we rotated the
pins so that all of the illegals got them, and they boarded the ship successfully without raising the suspicions of the British soldiers.

However, after our first day of sailing, the captain became very suspicious and informed the Jewish Agency that too much food was being consumed for the number of people that were supposed to be on
board. He also noticed that the dormitory was overcrowded. He con-
cluded that there were more than the thousand or so people declared
on the papers. The official from the Jewish Agency placated the captain's worries with gifts. The ship was uncomfortably crowded, the toilets were insufficient, the dormitory was vastly overcrowded with too
few saltwater showers, the food was poor and at times it was very hot.
Yet with our youth and high spirits, it was still a pleasant trip for us.

Our ship was the second legal ship to arrive in Haifa after the
war. Our first glimpse of Mount Carmel as we arrived in Haifa was

emotional, and we started singing "Hevenu shalom aleichem" ("We brought peace upon you") over and over again. I remember that because we arrived in the middle of Shabbat, we had to stay on the ship until after nightfall, which was very lucky for the illegals among us. This may have been arranged intentionally in order to give the illegals an opportunity to escape, under cover of darkness, the requisite checks on disembarkation.

Upon leaving the ship we were met by a herd of young people who roamed among us, slowing our exit and asking for the illegals so that they could extract them from the crowd. The British attempted to chase these young people away without success, and those affirming their illegal status were spirited away in the dark. We felt elated by the success of our illicit, benevolent activities and our cheating of the British quota of immigrants to Israel.

The British soldiers led us to the railway station to board a train to the Atlit detainee camp, where we underwent all the formalities: a health check, baggage and weapons check and identity paper check. For unknown reasons it took the British several days to process the new immigrants. Our stay in Atlit was uneventful, and we were restless with anticipation.

Kibbutz Life

Our group from Brussels was assigned to Kibbutz Amir, located in the Hula Valley in the Upper Galilee, close to Mount Hermon in the Golan Heights. A truck was sent from the kibbutz to pick us up. Climbing the slopes to the Upper Galilee after passing Tiberias was a new and strange experience for me. The barren land was full of black volcanic rocks called *bazelet*, basalt, an unusual and somewhat disturbing sight. I had never before seen such barren lands. It was September 1945, and the hot and dusty climate and landscape were very different from what I was used to. We arrived at the kibbutz at night, completely exhausted. We were greeted and fed well, and then we were shown to our quarters; I was to share with three others. In the morning I woke up to a view of Mount Hermon, and I dedicated the day to exploring the kibbutz.

In the centre of the kibbutz there was a community square, from which branched off many pathways that led to the various modest cottages and homes. Each cottage contained four to six small one-room apartments, each one with its own entrance and storage space — very simple accommodations by today's standards. The kibbutz was surrounded by eucalyptus trees, and around the cottages and along the walkways were manicured gardens. Our lodging was in the older wooden cottages, with either four bachelors or a married couple assigned to a room. The kibbutz schools and children's housing were located in the middle of the development. The children slept in their own housing complex and were picked up after school to spend recreational time with their parents. There was also a community dining room and adjacent kitchen, and a building with communal showers, where people often gathered after work to discuss the day's events and exchange ideas and opinions. Additionally, there were cattle sheds, a horse barn, a farm machinery shed and a woodworking plant, where the doors, windows and furniture for the kibbutz residences were manufactured. The kibbutz administrative offices were located at the base of a four-storey water tower that doubled as a communication tower, which used heliographs and electric light Morse code.

On the east side of the kibbutz, up a little hill just outside the residential area, was the doctor's office and living quarters, a pharmacy and a four-bed infirmary. The view of Mount Hermon from this hill was phenomenal, as the mountain changed colours with the shadows caused by the movement of the sun across the sky. I never tired of gazing at this majestic mountain.

Kibbutz Amir was an established community with its own administration. We were viewed as the nucleus for the growth and establishment of new kibbutzim and were being trained to manage and serve as administrators of a kibbutz. We were also learning various trades. We had one afternoon off a week to study and listen to discussions on politics, which included some propaganda and socialist indoctrination. There were about forty people in our group from all parts of Europe, such as Belgium, Switzerland (including refugees from Germany who had escaped to Belgium and Switzerland), Poland and the Balkan states. Most of our group was fluent in German or French, and some were fluent in both languages.

Our first week at the kibbutz was dedicated to orientation and acclimatization. Heads were chosen for the different divisions: dairy farming, fruit plantation, wheat farming, vegetable farming and so forth. I was assigned to the woodworking plant, which was my preference. Two permanent workers were allocated to this well-equipped plant, and I became the apprentice.

On some of our days off we were treated to excursions in the area. One of these trips was to one of the sources of the Jordan River, a picturesque spring surrounded by ancient trees located at the foot of Mount Hermon, where the water was about fifteen degrees Celsius even in the heat of summer. The Jordan River near Kibbutz Amir was also very cold, but we managed to overcome the cold and had a designated swimming area.

There were several kibbutzim in our area. To the north were Kibbutzim Dan and Dafna, and to the northeast were Kfar Szold and Shamir, both of which were at the foot of the Golan Heights. Lehavot Habashan, to the southeast, was a newer kibbutz that was built with our help. To the northwest were Kfar Giladi and Tel Hai, which were the two oldest Jewish settlements in the Hula Valley; they had been built on malaria-infested marsh and swampland and had been under attack by Arabs.

In the first month of our stay at Amir we encountered our first struggle with the British. A continuous flow of what the British considered illegal immigrants was coming through the Syrian border on foot. The British were convinced that a band of illegal immigrants had arrived the night before and were being hidden at Kfar Giladi. The British army surrounded Kfar Giladi and demanded access to the inhabitants in order to verify that they were legal. The kibbutz refused to allow the British army entry, and there was a standoff, with the British refusing to allow kibbutz inhabitants to leave or enter the property. A call went out to mobilize people from the surrounding settlements to encircle the British army. The response was immense, and the majority of the inhabitants from the surrounding settlements participated without the use of weapons. As time passed, the British did not know what to do. More and more people arrived from as far as Haifa and beyond. Thousands participated in the demonstration. Some British soldiers must have felt anxious at being blockaded by thousands of people, and they panicked. Shots were fired into the crowd, wounding a number of people. One of the wounded was a very good friend of mine from Belgium who was shot in the head and permanently lost some of his hearing as a result. The British finally surrendered and left their position without further confrontation.

Another confrontation in which I participated was between the British and Jewish settlers at Biriya, a community built on the mountaintop overlooking Safed. I'm not sure why, but despite the fact that the land had been paid for, the British army arrived early one morning and arrested all the inhabitants. An alarm went out, and the next week I, along with people from all over the north of Palestine, arrived at the foot of the mountain and climbed up to the settlement through the night. At the top, there was a breathtakingly beautiful view, and I watched the endless stream of people still climbing the mountain to join our cause. Eventually, the British soldiers guarding the settlement were overwhelmed by the sheer number of people confronting them and they left.

My stay at Kibbutz Amir and my time in the woodworking shop prepared me for a future where I would need to be self-sufficient. The trades of woodworking, building wooden roof frames and window and door installation supported me during my stay at the kibbutz and later, after my army service. I would also use these trades to build fortifications in the Negev desert during my army service in 1947. While at the kibbutz I also learned agricultural and fish farming. Agricultural farming was back-breaking work, and my experiences at the kibbutz gave me respect for the hard work of farmers and carpenters.

I admired the economic organization and social culture of the kibbutz. The community had a population of 150 families and various modern production facilities; it was a serious economic enterprise. The managerial competence of the kibbutz members was superior in all respects. We had many different orchards and grew bananas, grapes, apples, pears, oranges and other fruit. We also had different crops — wheat, corn and other vegetables — as well as cattle and dairy, chickens, eggs and fish ponds. The agricultural products required an assortment of farm machinery and the expertise to maintain it. In addition, there were groups responsible for building homes and furnishings.

The workforce consisted of every healthy adult living permanently or temporarily within the kibbutz. There was a work committee that delegated the available labourers to projects. The delegating committee had to be knowledgeable about the types of skills that were required for each job and designate the right person. It seemed to me that being a member of this work committee was a daunting task. The offices of the work committee were very animated, and after dinner I enjoyed observing their transactions. The managing members of the committee had no economic advantage but enjoyed the additional responsibilities that probably made their lives more interesting and varied, while providing some prestige. The responsibility was rotated among various members who wanted the extra challenge.

The workforce was divided among services such as education, childrearing, kitchen duties, washing and repairing. Certain tasks needed to be completed in a timely manner, and often two workforces were mobilized to complete a certain project, such as the harvest or concrete pouring for housing. I was often recruited for such tasks. The social needs of the community, such as health, recreation, cultural evenings and vacations, were delegated to another committee of people who enjoyed providing these activities.

My perspective on the kibbutz community and its success is that this form of social construct was a necessity of the time. The pioneers who arrived in Palestine in the 1920s had two major problems: employment and security. As individuals they could not get work because there was no capital base and infrastructure for employment. And their physical security could only be preserved in a collective by sharing expenses and labour. Agriculture was also the most practical resource for the kibbutz community to focus on. With time some of the kibbutzim grew and diversified into all kinds of industries, such as wood and metal industries, consumer goods, food processing and so on. The collectives lived very frugally and were able to build up capital and borrow money in sums that no individual family could have on its own. In this way they were able to acquire modern and efficient means of production and exploit production with economies of scale.

The kibbutz community was also strongly influenced by Eastern Europe's socialist movement; many national and military leaders were the product of this movement. They were mostly self-educated and had extraordinary self-discipline, and were well known for their achievements and influence. I foresaw that the kibbutz movement would eventually decline. As it turned out, the importance of kibbutzim diminished sharply over the years as a result of mass immigration to Israel. The means and needs of the modern state changed over time, and so did the goals of its population.

Every adult on the kibbutz was responsible for night watch duty. This meant walking around the perimeter of the kibbutz and the fish ponds and checking on the mounds of produce that were sometimes placed outside the kibbutz during harvest time. It was an eerie experience to walk alone in the middle of the night, listening to the jackals. We also received mandatory military training that would last for an afternoon, an evening or a whole day. This training was much more advanced than what had been offered by the French underground to its new recruits. Given my previous experience, I excelled at this training. We were exposed to and taught how to use all the light weaponry available to the Haganah: pistols, Lee-Enfield rifles, Sten submachine guns, Mills hand grenades, two-inch Israeli mortars and British Bren light machine guns. There was an ample mix of old and new arms from around the world that were left over from the battlefields of Europe. We also learned close hand-to-hand combat, including the use of sticks. There were also field exercises that taught us how to behave and manoeuvre in combat, including at night. Our instructor was the younger brother of Chaim Bar-Lev, who later became the chief of staff of the Israeli army and a cabinet minister for the Labour Party. He travelled from place to place on his motorcycle.

The military training offered by the kibbutz was considered an illegal activity by the British, but without this ongoing and intense training, Israel would have been destroyed during the war of 1948.

If we worked several Shabbats in a row, it was possible to get time off, and we could travel for two or three days. I used my time off to visit my mother in Hadera, where she rented a small apartment — one room plus a kitchen — from the Jewish Agency. I planted trees around her part of this six-apartment complex, which was only one floor high, so that she could have some shade on her roof to make the summer months more bearable. I was also permitted to use the kibbutz carpentry shop after hours to made my mother some basic furniture. Sometimes I visited my sister, Lea, in Kibbutz Ein HaHoresh, where she was attending high school, or my friends from Leipzig who had arrived in Israel before the war.

My mother made her living as a seamstress. She mostly worked from her home in Hadera but sometimes worked from other people's homes. She also taught sewing in Ein HaHoresh, where my sister lived. She was greatly appreciated by the people in the villages and in Hadera, and she became good friends with many of her customers.

When we travelled to Tel Aviv or Haifa, we were required to leave the kibbutz by 4:00 a.m. in order to catch a ride with the delivery trucks that brought kibbutz products to the city markets. The drivers were excellent, and the panoramic view as we descended from the Upper Galilee to Tiberias beside the Sea of Galilee was breathtaking in the early morning.

Living on a kibbutz required us to give up much of our individuality. I believe that we all went through the same self-doubt when it came to the loss of our identities in exchange for the good of the community. We had to relinquish the ability to make many of our own decisions about work, personal plans and desires to the kibbutz committee. The committee had the last say as to what an individual's plans were going to be, using the interests of the entire community as a measure. The process was somewhat subjective, and with so many approaches, opinions and different understandings, the loss of some of my self-determination was very difficult to get used to. Not only was the kibbutz mired in the process of making decisions for its individual members, it also had the task of reaching decisions for its collective future. Even if the ends were agreed upon by the committee members, there still needed to be a consensus on the means. Not all the kibbutz members were enamored with farm work and its harsh physical demands. Some members dreamed of academic and professional careers in medicine, engineering, architecture, journalism, teaching, flying and art. Some members left the kibbutz and were successful in realizing their dreams in their later years, despite all odds.

~

A group of us at Kibbutz Amir had the idea of starting our own kibbutz in Ramat HaSharon. At that time it was a small village that supplied vegetables to Tel Aviv. This location was selected because of all the work opportunities it offered us. I was elected secretary over our discussions, which we held during evening sessions. I enjoyed this duty and discharged it well. The leaders of Kibbutz HaArzi, the kibbutz movement of Hashomer Hatzair, proposed to have our group unite with another one that had emigrated from Egypt. Two other people and I were chosen to visit the Egyptian group at their kibbutz and report back about the possibility of a merger. We visited the kibbutz for a week and had the gruelling job of removing stones from the fields. The Egyptian group spoke Hebrew, French, Arabic and English. Some individuals also spoke German, Serbian and Polish. Hebrew was the common language, though some of us spoke it better than others. At my father's insistence, I'd had to learn Hebrew as a child, and now it served me well as I was able to advance more quickly in the language than some of the others.

Eventually a group of us moved to Ramat HaSharon and united with the group of pioneers from Egypt. We numbered over one hundred members in total. Our complex was composed of some barracks, which were used for the public spaces, the kitchen and the dining hall, and we lived in tents with two to four people per tent, depending on the tent's size and the marital status of the individuals. We lived very simply, eating basic food and using boxes as furniture. Our money was saved for the eventual settlement and for building our future. We supplied our own entertainment. Every evening someone would play the piano while we sang or danced, sometimes late into the night.

Ramat HaSharon was very agricultural at that time, and many of our members went to work for vegetable farmers and in orange groves in the area. I worked in a woodworking plant. One unforgettable experience, which I used to describe to my own employees later on, occurred when I was a new employee at Kibbutz Glil Yam, near our complex. I was assigned the task of assembling doors to make them ready to glue together. It was my first day on the job, and I gave it my very best effort, wanting to satisfy the manager. By the end of the day, I was exhausted. The manager passed by and asked me how many doors I was able to prepare. I answered with pride that I had completed ten. He then dryly commented that twenty-two to twenty-four was the norm. In that moment I hated him intensely for not appreciating what I believed to be a heroic effort. I went home feeling bitter, disappointed and brooding. The next day I must have completed fifteen doors, but I very distinctly remember reaching the twenty-two to twenty-four door norm after several days, and I was much less tired than I had been on the first day. I realized that objectivity is sometimes not possible. This was one lesson I remembered for life.

After a while, the opportunity presented itself for me to work as a roof framer for Solel Boneh, the big building contractor owned by the Histadrut, the trade union organization. I made good money for the kibbutz and the three to four people working with me, and we became an excellent crew. We were able to anticipate each other's needs before those needs were expressed. One of my crew members became an architect; another became a stage director at Habima Theatre.

It is beyond my understanding where I got the strength to do hard physical labour day after day without rest. Being young must have helped. By the middle of 1946, I was voted to be the security chief and future commander of the kibbutz. I was sent off to complete a course for commanders. The first four weeks of the course took place in a big established kibbutz near Ra'anana. The course was dedicated to teaching us how to overcome obstacles by increasing our physical capacity through exposure to various military sports. One of the instructors was Ariel Sharon. Although he was also a student, he was already an instructor as well. During one of the training sessions, Ariel had us jump from a two-storey building from all sorts of positions — sitting, standing, dangling from the ledge. First we had to jump without equipment and then with equipment. This intense exercise caused torn ligaments in my knees. It was extremely painful, and the next day I was unable to stand.

After this phase of the course, we all received a two-week vacation. I returned home and received medical attention for my knees. The remainder of the commander's course continued at Kibbutz Beit Keshet in the Lower Galilee, right at the foot of Mount Tabor. Ariel Sharon was in my group again, but this time just as a student. He was an excellent student with enormous brute strength. The commander of this course was a mature man, close to fifty years old. We conducted our demanding exercises day and night. It was difficult for me because my torn ligaments had not yet healed completely, but I was determined to persist, and I was also given some consideration for my injury. We were also trained in crisis decision making and problem solving as well as in instructing others.

For three months we underwent intensive training. During this time we also had the opportunity to explore the Lower Galilee, from the heights of Mount Tabor to the Sea of Galilee, including Tiberias, and we discovered mountains and fields, Jewish villages and Arab villages, large and small.

When I returned to the kibbutz, I started organizing our security.

In the United Nations, discussions on the Palestine issue were already in full swing. There were constant clashes between Arabs and Jews at the border of Tel Aviv and Jaffa and other hot spots. There was awareness of the potential for immediate and high conflict. I was responsible for acquiring what were considered by the British illegal arms, mostly from the Haganah. I succeeded in purchasing handguns from some prostitutes, who had received them from pilots as payment for their services. It was lucrative for pilots to smuggle weapons into Palestine. We had to find good hiding places for the weapons that would also allow us to access them easily. Some of us started to sleep with weapons. It was my responsibility to train all members of the kibbutz in proper arms handling. Training took place over many weeks, each time with a different group of about twelve members. I was also assigned by the Haganah to train new immigrants, young and not so young.

We trained in the fields day and night, and I taught the use of the different types of arms, most of which were of British origin and often classified as obsolete. Nevertheless, we had no choice but to use what was available. It was my responsibility to organize the training, and I was given absolute authority as to the structure of the sessions. Once in a while I was provided with a training location, but most of the time I had to devise my own guard system to warn against British intrusion. The exercises took place in fields, small forests, orange groves, orange-packing sheds and empty stables. Occasionally I was provided with a pickup truck for transporting the trainees. I enjoyed the high esteem that went with the position of instructor.

At the end of each training session there was a live ammunition and grenade-throwing exercise. These exercises caused me extreme anxiety. They were very noisy and involved individuals who had no military experience, and we had to be on guard not to be discovered and trapped by the British. I was pleased that during the several years I conducted weapons training and exercises, not one person in any of my groups received a single injury.

The Negev

In September 1947 I was with a group of about thirty other people that was directed to go to the Negev region in the south. The Jewish Agency negotiated a budget to pay us for preparing the arid soil for forestation and for guards for the first year. The kibbutz we were sent to was about sixteen kilometres south of Beersheba, just west of the main highway through Beersheba, Bir 'Asluj and El Arish. It was in the middle of arid, sandy dunes, partially covered in rock and blessed with only a thin layer of sand. The barracks and what we called the security or safe house, a two-storey building made of concrete, and the double security fence were already in place. I was now the commander of this location and the people there. But a kibbutz does not work like an army: it has a more democratic and social structure, and I was an elected member of this institution. Every decision had to pass the scrutiny of the various committees and occasionally all the members. The vote, not strict command, was the order of the day. It was a membership of volunteers, not conscripted individuals, so everyone had the option of leaving. Criticism and dissent were frequent, especially when unusual effort and risk were involved.

I started exploring the barren terrain of the area by foot, usually with the company of about twelve armed men. It was difficult to orient myself in the new terrain, yet I managed well. The Bedouin were the predominant population of the area but we rarely encountered them. Our supplies came from our kibbutz in Ramat HaSharon. Our water came from Beit Eshel, a kibbutz two kilometres southeast of Beersheba. We had a truck with a water tank, and a pump would send the water up to another tank on top of a two-storey building. From there the water would flow to the faucets that had been installed — a rather primitive instalment, but it met our needs.

We had to swear in a dozen of our people as assistant police officers so that we would have legal bearers of arms according to the British to accompany our water truck. In addition, we had hidden weapons in waterproof envelopes in the water tank. We also had a wireless Morse code machine, and we communicated at preplanned spots at timed intervals, two to four times a day. Only the operator, Bumi, and I were authorized to be in the room with the machine, which was located in the concrete building of the kibbutz. Arms and military training for members continued on a regular basis as did the building of fortifications around the 100- by 120-metre perimeter of the kibbutz.

Shortly before the historic November 1947 UN decision dividing Palestine and establishing the State of Israel, we were advised by wireless to increase our safety detachment of trucks and instructed that no vehicle was to travel to the south alone. We were also provided with a tractor-bulldozer and two tractor operators to help us fortify the kibbutz, and I was given instructions on how to do that from the Haganah engineering department. All of our people were busy digging trenches and defence positions. Sandbags were used to protect the roofs of the defence bunker, and other installations were continually improved during the last months of 1947 and the beginning of 1948.

In November 1947 our water truck was sent to Beit Eshel with a pickup truck carrying ten men for protection, as recommended by the Haganah. On their way back from Beit Eshel they were ambushed.

The pickup truck was hit and went up in flames. The water truck was riddled with holes. All of the men returned to the kibbutz, but three of them were seriously injured. We had no medical help at that time and did not have the ability to treat them. As we debated how to assist our wounded men, three British armoured vehicles arrived at our fence and we had to hide our illegal wireless and weapons. I remembered that there was a Bren machine gun out in the open and someone hid it under the mattress of one of the wounded men. Two other men and I met with the British officers and recognized them as being from the Arab Legion, which we considered our enemy. They told us that they had heard about the ambush and that they were there to investigate the incident and assist us. This put us in a very difficult position. Once inside the kibbutz they requested permission to use our wireless to communicate with their headquarters. We stood there with poker faces and told them that we did not have a wireless. The British officers said that they didn't believe us because they had been able to tap into our communications, despite the fact that we changed radio frequency codes frequently. Nevertheless we were adamant that we did not have the equipment, and so they had to return to their vehicles to take care of their communications.

When the soldiers returned from their vehicle, they offered to transport our wounded to the hospital in Beersheba. We now had another problem; the hospital was staffed by Arabs in what was then an exclusively Arab town. And because of the presence of the British soldiers, we couldn't use our wireless to seek advice on how to best assist our wounded. As the security chief, I debated the issue and possible outcomes with two other members of the kibbutz, and we decided to take an enormous chance and send the wounded men to Beersheba with the British soldiers. We knew that they had no chance of surviving if they remained at the kibbutz without medical care. After the British left, we communicated with the Haganah command centre and told them what had happened. Later we were told that our men had arrived at the hospital in Beersheba, had received first aid there and were then transported by ambulance to our hospital in Nir Am. They were later transferred to a Tel Aviv hospital for additional care. All this was an enormous burden on me. We were all frustrated by the fact that we were isolated and had no medical help. We complained to the Haganah and demanded that medical facilities be made available to us immediately.

After this we received additional barbed wire and land mines with instructions on how to lay them out and a visiting engineer to advise me. I was allowed to apply my judgment to implement the plans, but I had only one trained person to lay them out. Since installing the mines would have taken much too long with only one person, and because I had previous training, I also participated in laying out the land mines, though I was advised not to. Regrettably, my trained land mine specialist set a mine off and lost a leg and an arm. I was the only one left to complete the task and placed mines at the point where vehicles might approach the kibbutz. While I was laying the mines, six Jeeps approached. I alerted the whole kibbutz as the vehicles neared the long and protected entrance. I was ready to activate the mines, only to recognize in time that they were Haganah vehicles, heavily armed with two machine guns mounted on each and supplied with additional arms and mortars. This was my first encounter with Chaim Bar-Lev, who was then a battalion commander.

~

The months after the attack on our water truck were very difficult, as the only water remaining in the truck was what was level with the lowest hole on the tank, which was not very much. Our supplies were not delivered to us until after the November 29, 1947, UN declaration of partition. We could move only in protected convoys, which still necessitated breaching of British and Arab-held territory. The British were duplicitous and gave our positions and schedules to the Arabs, so we had to find ways to mislead the British. There were many battles on the supply routes, and so the Haganah went on the offensive in order to clear those routes from constant attacks on our trucks and supplies.

During this time, for at least three months, we lived on emergency rations of difficult-to-digest crackers, matzahs, sardines, condensed milk and beans. We also rationed water to only two cups per person per day. Luckily it was winter and the rainy season, though there is not much rain in the Negev. When it did rain we collected all the water we could from the roofs of the barracks. Some of us would use the opportunity to wash ourselves outdoors while half naked.

In the months of January to April, sandstorms are frequent in the Negev, and when these storms occur there is nowhere to hide. Sand enters everywhere: the kitchen, the food, beds, eyes, noses, mouths and ears. No matter how tightly you try to cover up, the very fine sand of this region will enter. This phenomenon, coupled with our limited water supply, made this a challenging time. We also did not believe we had enough people to defend our position. But the authorities at the Haganah did not consider it necessary to send us reinforcements.

Because of illness and other reasons our numbers dwindled to only twenty-eight. Morale was low; there was a deep feeling of isolation. Our kibbutz at Ramat HaSharon negotiated with the Jewish Agency to increase our budget and bring more recruits. One day Chaim Bar-Lev visited us and inquired about rumours that we were going to abandon the kibbutz. I knew nothing of this and had no answer, but the Jewish Agency did increase our budget and sent us seven or eight more people. This slight increase in membership was an enormous boost to our morale.

By March 1948, the Haganah forces in our region had become more substantial. We now had steady patrols of two or three armoured trucks. Israeli-produced, they had a peculiar, easily recognizable appearance, and their presence made us feel much less isolated. One night we were even visited by a troupe of entertainers and musicians from the Palmach known as the Chizbatron. They became very famous during the War of Independence. Most of the actors in this group remained famous after the war and joined various well-established theatre groups.

Because of the armoured vehicles I was told that we could prepare our water truck for a run to fetch a supply of water from Revivim, about fifteen kilometres due south of us but about twenty kilometres en route through the desert. A fierce desert sandstorm arose on the day selected for the run, but it had to be completed, storm or not. With our water truck in the middle of a convoy of armoured trucks, we made our way slowly through the sometimes difficult route. I sat at the front of the first truck to scout for possible mines, a challenging task in good weather but near impossible in the sandstorm, where visibility was no more than a metre ahead of us. We were lucky on this run, and we managed to make two trips with the water truck. And so our water problem was alleviated for a while.

Sometime in the middle of March, on a very beautiful day, I decided to go out to scout the surroundings. Because of the sun and wonderful spring weather, I completely ignored the fact that we were in a war zone. I sat enjoying the weather and the nature around me, oblivious to the dangers, when shots suddenly started to rain down on me. With some difficulty, I succeeded in returning to the kibbutz without any injuries, but exhausted from the physical and mental stress. I had to report the incident to my superior, and it was no surprise that I was severely reprimanded for my carelessness.

The next morning the regional commander arrived at our kibbutz with a full company and three armoured trucks. He asked me to join him with a group of ten of my men for a demonstration of how to complete a successful reconnaissance. It was common sense that a mission would be more successful with armoured trucks and ammunition than it had been with just me, alone, with no ammunition. But once we entered about four kilometres within Arab territory, we were fired upon from every direction, but were able to escape, using the trucks for cover. The regional commander reassembled his forces and went back to his base. Any field activity, especially under fire, is extremely exhausting and so all the participants went to rest for the remainder of the day.

After some time, the observation team informed me that there was heavy activity in the hills surrounding us. Looking through my binoculars, I was startled by the intensity of activity that I observed. At a distance I could see many trucks filled with people and Bedouin on horseback galloping back and forth. It was difficult to come to any conclusions about their intentions, but an attack seemed to be an imminent possibility. I immediately connected with the regional commander who had been with us earlier, and he contacted Chaim Bar-Lev. As I listened in on the conversation, it seemed to me that the commander was exaggerating the danger somewhat. Bar-Lev took the situation very seriously; he quickly arrived at our kibbutz with a number of empty trucks and some reinforcements. He left only one group of twelve men and some additional weapons and repeated this manoeuvre three more times. I believe he made it appear as though we were supported by hundreds of defenders. We were only forty-seven people but comforted by the additional firepower. The misleading manoeuvre worked, and except for some far-away futile shots, we were not attacked. The crisis calmed down; by the third day, we could see the Arab forces on the hill thinning out, and by the fourth day they were gone. We were elated by the outcome of this tactic.

I was sent to Ramat HaSharon and Tel Aviv to plead our case for the recruitment of more people to our kibbutz. Arriving in Tel Aviv with a handgun and two grenades under my leather jacket was strange, especially when passing British soldiers or policemen. My mother had moved to Tel Aviv in the fall of 1947 and was renting a one-room apartment in the Hatikva neighbourhood, a working-class area. She had not liked living in rural Hadera. In her small apartment, she started producing dresses that she sold in Tel Aviv stores. The dresses sold well and she had the respect of her clients. I had not seen her for many months, so I went to visit her immediately after arriving in Tel Aviv. The sounds of sirens and gunfire were loud in this area of southern Tel Aviv, which was not too distant from the border between Arab and Jewish territory.

The negotiations for additional personnel went very well and we were promised a reinforcement of people shortly. In the meantime, I struggled with the traffic, noise and activity in Tel Aviv. Living in the isolated and desolate Negev for more than half a year had made me very sensitive to the bustle of the city. It was ironic given that I had previously lived in the most cosmopolitan cities in the world. After a few days I returned to the meeting place for the convoys. Every person who wanted to join the convoy was assigned a truck with no questions asked, and we departed early in the morning.

As promised by the command, shortly after my return to the kibbutz we were sent about twenty young men to reinforce our membership. All between seventeen and eighteen years old, they were Polish-born survivors of the concentration camps and forests of Eastern Europe. They had just finished three or four weeks of basic military training. I started immediately with intensive training in and around our home base. They integrated very well with us and there were no social problems to speak of. We now boasted about sixty-five men, and our morale was boosted further.

~

In the spring of 1948 the tensions increased. The Haganah was busy creating a secure territory from where it would be possible to fight the threat of invasion from the surrounding Arab armies.

One day, a very low-flying Dakota passed over our kibbutz. We prepared to respond in case it passed over again. It did fly over again and we fired at it with two machine guns before receiving a wire informing us that the plane was ours. Luckily we had not damaged the plane. It was exciting to know that we had a new plane to assist us with transportation and supplies. New armaments from Czechoslovakia also arrived. We heard that combat airplanes similar to Messerschmitts had been obtained, and we received new Mauser rifles and

MG machine guns used by the Germans during World War II. Now I had the task of training our people to use the new guns. I was familiar with these weapons from my time in the French underground, where we had confiscated these arms from the Germans on many occasions and had used them with great proficiency. Based on my experience, and following the structure and directions of our prepared training materials, I wrote a training manual for both the MG and Mauser, which I and others used in the region for some time after this.

An Egyptian-born, university-educated member of our kibbutz was assigned to the headquarters of Chaim Bar-Lev to listen to radio transmissions from the Egyptian army and gather critical information about the timing and size of the invasion. He was able to tell us that the Egyptian army would invade on or before May 15, 1948. On May 14, David Ben-Gurion declared the establishment of the State of Israel, and on May 15 the surrounding Arab armies invaded. The invasion advanced rapidly on all fronts, and the Egyptians took possession of Beersheba, which was dotted with British Taggart forts, military police forts. The newly assembled planes, flown by pilots who had never commanded these types of aircraft before, succeeded in stopping the Egyptians' advances at various points.

Chaim Bar-Lev arrived and established a command post for an operation to conquer Bir 'Asluj, about five kilometres from Revivim, where a fort had been occupied by the Egyptians. The troops assembled in Revivim and departed in the dark of the very early morning hours with the hope of surprising the Egyptians. However, the surprise factor was lost when a few mines were triggered on the road to the fort. One Jeep exploded, and we suffered the first casualties of this battle. The attack did not go so well. With the darkness of night quickly approaching, the leader requested permission to retreat. However, permission was denied, and an order was given to reassemble and attack from a different direction. To everyone's surprise, the fort gave way. The Egyptians remaining in the fort came out and surrendered.

Before the attack the participants were briefed that under no circumstances were they to enter the fort after a successful mission. The fear was that it was booby-trapped with explosives that would be detonated with the victors inside. Intoxicated with the thrill of victory, a group of our combatants entered the fort. To be fair they also wanted to check if any Egyptian fighters remained inside. As feared, the fort was detonated by an Egyptian officer who was hiding at a distance. He was immediately captured. Fourteen of our fighters were injured, some fatally. One of our fighters was a female first-aid nurse and teacher from Kibbutz Ein Harod. She courageously scrambled into the rubble of the fort and removed each of the fourteen men herself. The Egyptian prisoners were checked for hidden arms and then confined in a camp surrounded by barbed wire.

This operation and a later one taught me the necessity of forward and backup command posts in military, as well as corporate, operations. The men in the front command post are influenced by casualties and by the shifts in battle and so have difficulty staying objective. The men in the backup command have a much greater ability to gather information and analyze the situation objectively.

The conquest of the Taggart fort at Bir 'Asluj brought with it a period of feverish activity. The fort was surrounded by an abundance of building materials not available in the Negev at this time: wood, corrugated metal sheets, barbed wire, steel posts, etc. Every kibbutz in the area was notified that these materials were available to use in fortifying their defences. The route between the kibbutz and the fort was under our control now, and we sent our truck there for several pickup runs. We used the new supplies to build underground bunkers and to fortify all our defence positions within our barbed wire fences.

As time passed and other battles ensued, the demands and pressures of combat affected everyone who was in a position of command. There were not enough resources to go around, and we were all pushed to our absolute limit. I also requested one or two weeks off so that I could go north for a rest, as others had done. The regional commander's response was that everyone accepting responsibility had to give more and expect less, that this pressure just came with being in command. But being under the constant scrutiny of the kibbutz members was taking its toll on me, and I wanted to quit and join the Eighth Battalion of the Negev Brigade.

After much negotiating with the territorial commander, I was offered a temporary position replacing the Moshav Nevatim commander for two weeks, after which he would let me have some time off in the north. The main difference between a kibbutz and a moshav is that every family in the moshav has their own home and a small field, with the bigger fields being worked communally. Because of its residential structure, a moshav was larger than a kibbutz, making it much more difficult to defend and to guard at night. Moshav Nevatim was about eight kilometres east of Beersheba. A platoon was formed to get to the moshav by circumventing Beersheba from the south by foot. The whole unit was brought close to the southwest border of Beersheba after nightfall, and from there we marched about twelve kilometres with all of our equipment, including machine guns and munitions, to Moshav Nevatim. The situation at the moshav was that the civilians wanted to leave, and since their request was not granted, they declared a strike. This might have been why we were now there with a platoon and commander. I tried to do what I could under the circumstances and spoke with the inhabitants to try to get their cooperation. This worked more or less, but it did not help me in my quest for relaxation.

One morning, the moshav's original commander arrived in a Piper aircraft. I strenuously protested his request that I be his permanent replacement and commanded the pilot to fly me to Nir Am, the command centre of the Negev. The pilot didn't know whether to obey me or the original Moshav commander, so he asked the people nearby who was in command. Everyone said that I was. And so the pilot took off with me as his passenger. As I landed in Nir Am, I noticed that

Chaim Bar-Lev was returning from an observation trip and requested a meeting with him. Sitting at the entrance of his tent, I overheard his discussions with several commanders who were requesting additional people, materials and equipment. Bar-Lev explained patiently to everyone that given his budget, he could do nothing more and that allocating his reserves to any one unit would be to the detriment of the entire defence forces. My encounter with Bar-Lev was very short. I explained to him the agreement that I'd had with the regional commander of the south, and Bar-Lev gave me a voucher and a permit to fly out that same evening on a Dakota transport plane.

As I waited at the landing strip, a Jeep arrived and my name was called out. I was told that I had to return to meet with Bar-Lev who then told me that he could not let me go because the regional commander of the south had demanded that I return to him first. I was then assigned the task of commanding a platoon of thirty-five men to protect about ten engineers who were to check roads and sweep them for mines. I was promised that after I finished this task, I could take my much-needed break. Although I was not pleased, I understood that no one else was available to do this job. The next morning I started my trip by convoy to Nirim, where the regional commander of the south was located.

The platoon went out with an armoured truck and deployed into the hills to monitor the area for dangerous activity and ensure the safety of the engineers as they did their job sweeping for mines. The job was completed in three days, and I finally received my pass for rest in the more populated north.

After this short break I went to the Eighth Battalion, which was in Be'er Ya'akov, in central Israel. All of the officers and staff were friends and acquaintances of mine, including the unit commander, Joseph Ribkind. I expressed my desire to join this battalion, and I was received enthusiastically. I was immediately taken to the recruiting camp, where I was told that since I was just returning from the

Negev now, my commencement date with the battalion would be that day. Only later did I understand the implications for me. My date of mobilization became May 1948 rather than 1947. It disturbed me in the coming years that I did not receive credit for my prior service, as this later mobilization date postponed my discharge from the army. Explanations and signatures from the battalion commander, brigade commander and others in command did not change this.

Final Battles

Stationed at Be'er Ya'akov, the Eighth Battalion was really only a skeleton at this point. A long stay in the Negev had caused steady attrition. Its soldiers were well-trained and well-educated, and all of them had been promoted up and out of the battalion to become officers in the army, air force and navy. Additionally, there had been illness and fatalities within the battalion. In actuality the Eighth Battalion was without soldiers, but it had a framework of unit officers, a communications unit and NCOs, as well as other experienced personnel. Headquarters decided that instead of liquidating the battalion, they would replenish it. In the meantime battalion members were sent to different courses to improve their skills. I was sent to an intensive three-month course to learn how to use the heavier machine guns.

When I returned to Be'er Ya'akov, nothing had changed. There were still no soldiers to train or instruct, so my fellow officers and I went to Tel Aviv every evening for the next two or three weeks. One evening around the end of September 1948, the company's sergeant major told us that no one was permitted to leave the camp. Twenty of us left the camp anyway, as there was nothing else to do there in the evening. At about midnight, Jeeps and command cars raced through the streets of Tel Aviv, with soldiers entering every movie theatre, café and entertainment spot, shouting, "All members of the Negev Brigade out!" A majority of the brigade was collected and ferried to trucks, which were filled with the AWOL soldiers by 2:00 a.m. Back at Be'er Ya'akov we were greeted with a huge surprise. The barracks were filled with new soldiers who had come straight from the first recruit-training camp. They were sleeping on the floors without blankets, as no one had been there to receive them. Complete confusion had been caused by the absence of the junior officers and NCOS of the battalion.

In the morning we were told that we were all to be mobilized in the Negev that night. No excuses were allowed despite the short notice. I was assigned a group of strangers, and as their commander, had to prepare them for mobilization and look out for their well-being. By lunchtime, I got permission to take my group out for a live shooting exercise so that I could get a sense of their capabilities. All preparations were completed in a rush.

By nightfall our buses arrived to transport us to the Negev, but we were not finished with our preparations. The boxes for the Mills hand grenades were opened and the grenades assembled and distributed while we were on the move in overcrowded buses — a definite safety issue. The buses arrived well after nightfall at Moshav Be'er Tuvia, a short distance north of the Taggart fort of Iraq Suwaydan, which was occupied by the Egyptians. The Egyptians controlled the coastal route to Hebron and the route from Beersheba to Jerusalem, keeping this area in the southern part of Israel isolated from the rest of the country. Our march started, and we were soon in the midst of Egyptian-held territory. Some of the soldiers started to fall back. There was much to carry: mortars, guns, ammunition, grenades. As our march continued, I had to ensure that we were safe and that we did not leave any individuals behind. It was extremely difficult to convince inexperienced soldiers of the need to keep in line with the rest of the group and to make them understand the dangers of falling behind. And I had to do this without raising my voice and making any untoward noises. Some of the stronger members of our platoon helped those who were weaker. A short time before daybreak we arrived at the hills of Bror Hayil, where we set up our encampment. My platoon shared a hill with another platoon that was led by my commander. The soldiers we relieved were experienced and battle-tested members of the Yiftach Brigade. These soldiers were to start the offensive two or three days later.

It was late October and the nights were cold. We were not properly dressed for the weather. I suffered severe rheumatic pain in my shoulders and legs and had difficulty commanding such an inexperienced group of soldiers. Some of the soldiers wandered away to explore the immediate surroundings, and one of them detonated a mine. Our doctor happened to be nearby and took charge. Two of the new soldiers called to me and showed me two very dangerous mines that they had picked up. These mines were of the sort that sprang a metre into the air before exploding. I was horrified, but in the calmest voice that I could manage, I advised the soldiers that they must very slowly and carefully place the mines back on the ground. It seemed like an eternity before they finally understood the grave peril they were in and did as they were told.

We had at our disposal some powerful weapons and munitions, and training started immediately. We could not use live ammunition for the exercises, but we worked hard to improve the untrained soldiers' handling of weapons. Since I was now second-in-command, I made it a rule to attend to all worries while I was awake but to sleep well once I entered my sleeping bag, leaving all worries to my commander, who had taken charge.

Late into the third morning of our encampment on the hill, a convoy of our trucks stopped at the Egyptian checkpoint as agreed upon in a ceasefire agreement. The convoy was supposed to bring supplies to the south. From the hills, we could observe the convoy as it began to move south through the Egyptian lines. All of a sudden, we observed soldiers running out of two trucks just before they exploded. Minutes later all hell broke loose. Three low-flying World War II British planes launched torpedo-like bombs into the

Egyptian-occupied Taggart fort. As night fell, all the Egyptian-occupied hills along the east-west route were attacked. But the more critical ones — Iraq Suwaydan, Lachish and Beit Guvrin — were not hit. I listened all night to the battle transmissions on our communication apparatus. At times I even spoke to the Egyptian operator in French, attempting to distract him. It was a game of cat and mouse, trying to follow the channels of communication in order to hear the progress of the battle. It was also heartbreaking to hear about the failures, the appeals for help, the difficulties of retreat and the evacuation of casualties and fatalities.

In the morning we saw the Egyptians heading eastward to Lachish or Beit Guvrin with their cannons and heavier equipment. I had been left in charge, and I immediately contacted the battalion commander and requested permission to fire at the Egyptians. Permission was emphatically denied, and I was told that I was not to dare use the soldiers that I had with me in such combat. I was asked what I would do if the Egyptians decided to storm the hill. I disagreed with the battalion commander and later wrote about the incident, without naming people or places, in the military journal *Maarachot*, which was dedicated to military strategic problems. The story was published with the conclusion that only in rare cases should a battalion commander provide direct communications to higher echelons, in this case the brigade commander.

Every evening from then on, attacks were carried out against the Egyptian fortifications. Beersheba was attacked and taken by the Haganah forces. So, slowly, one Egyptian fortification after another was successfully claimed. The Negev was now open and unified with the north. Our base on the hills became unnecessary, and we were sent back to Be'er Ya'akov to start training the new soldiers. The successful operation to free the Negev from Egyptian control and unite it with the north was called Mivtza Yo'av, Operation Yo'av.

~

The soldiers assigned to my platoon were all born in Poland and had survived the war in Tashkent and other Soviet republics. They were very experienced in survival and were full of vitality and humour. Later I would hear their stories and learn about the corruption and mismanagement within the Soviet Union. The mortar platoon was overwhelmingly staffed by new immigrants from Romania, and the explosive platoon by immigrants from China, the majority of them from Shanghai, where their Russian parents had fled after the Russian Revolution. Our motto was *ein breirah*, "there is no choice," and this motto helped all of us to overcome many hardships.

Our battalion returned to Be'er Ya'akov and to our regular routine, which included an early wake-up call, physical training and long-distance running; we were then required to clean the barracks before having breakfast. The rest of our day was dedicated to weapons and equipment training. After some routine weeks, I was assigned an encampment on a fortified hill across from the hills the Egyptians had captured along the Gaza Strip. As the commander, I organized sporting events and competitions on the side of the hill that was out of sight of the Egyptians. My aim was to keep my soldiers from succumbing to the boredom inherent in waiting for battle or commands from above. We also organized some evening entertainment and Shabbat services with songs and candle lighting. After three weeks we returned to our base. On my return I received commendations from our battalion commander for maintaining the morale of my platoon.

In March 1949 the Negev Brigade and another brigade formed a force to conquer Um al-Rashrash, today known as Eilat, which was occupied by the Jordanians. This territory was deemed to be part of Palestine and had been accorded to the Jewish state by the UN in the 1947 Partition Plan. The Jordanians withdrew as we approached. This campaign, called Operation Uvda, was considered to be the last military operation of Israel's War of Independence.

Over the next few months, I was responsible for six heavy machine guns placed in different camps, and I could choose to stay in any of the six locations. I also had enough free time to write a lengthy article — which was published in *Bamahane* (*In the Camp*), the army's weekly journal — on the topic of how the army could develop the land in this area and also help relieve the boredom of the soldiers.

The camp in Eilat had the enormous advantage of having a beach where we could sleep and take dips in the cool water. There were also earth huts where the temperature was more comfortable than in the tents. However, the disadvantage of staying in Eilat was the strong hot winds that came from the east, from the deserts of Transjordan, and often caused nasty sandstorms.

My battalion was later sent back to Beit Guvrin, south of Jerusalem. Located on the Beersheba-to-Jerusalem route, Beit Guvrin was now to be the headquarters of our battalion. It was also the site of a British Taggart fort. The landscape there consisted of mountains, vegetation, small and large rocks and caves — very different from what we had seen in the Negev. I was placed in the village of Duwayma, near Hebron. Initially, the village was quiet, and I had the additional responsibility of supervising the machine guns in other units.

By chance, one day I was at our headquarters when the commander told a friend of mine who was also present that he needed his assistance for a mission into enemy territory. My friend responded that he was extremely tired from all of the demands placed on him. When I heard this, I volunteered my services for the mission. The company went out the next morning with three platoons, totalling one hundred men from different units. I stayed in front of the mixed platoon that was under my charge, and after about half an hour I was directed to establish a presence on a certain mountain. I had no idea where the others were going to be placed. Once we settled on the mountain, it did not take long to attract intense gunfire from all around us. The company commander called my field communication device to tell me that he and his platoon had been ambushed and asked that I come to his assistance. I told him that we were also under fire, and he advised me to remain where I was. After a while,

I decided that we would descend the mountain on the side where we were not experiencing any fire. Unfortunately, at the same time, the enemy started to ascend the mountain on that same side, and we suffered many casualties. The third platoon was positioned on a hill across from ours. They were also leaving their position, noticed our situation and did their best to cover our descent.

We met at the bottom of the mountain, and I took over the command. Suddenly we noticed that we were in a minefield. Given my experience with mines, I knew that we were safest if we walked on the ridges of soil where there was rainfall runoff, as the runoff eroded the soil and exposed part of the mines. I told the men not to move until I moved and to follow behind me in a single file with a distance of at least one metre between each man. My eyes were completely focused on the path as I advanced slowly and methodically. Finally, we reached the village, surviving the minefield without incident. I reported the series of events to the battalion commander who then organized a force to return to the area in a hurry. Some of the men who had followed me out of danger volunteered to return to guide the force. A small plane was also ordered to assist. Before the force was sent out I had to write a detailed report.

After the fact, we learned that this mission was supposed to have had four companies as well as air support. However, on the morning of the mission there were low clouds in the sky, so the air force decided to postpone the mission. The message about the postponement had reached every company scheduled to participate except ours, the company caught in the ambush. The families of some of the fallen came to talk with me, asking me questions that were extremely difficult to answer. It was one of the hardest experiences of my life; I was alive, yet their loved ones were not. It was all the more difficult to bear the losses when we knew that the fighting was close to an end, and especially when the casualties could have been avoided. We spent about one month in this area before returning to Be'er Ya'akov.

~

Whenever we got some vacation time, we were provided with a truck that would transport us to various entertainment venues. Those who had families usually went to visit them, and others returned to their moshav or kibbutz. I used to visit my mother in her small apartment in Tel Aviv. Since I couldn't ask my hard-working mother for money, I used every opportunity I had to look for extra work. There were three woodworking shops located side by side in Rishon LeZion, and I often went there in search of work. I was warmly received and generously compensated, as I was able to work well with the machinery in the shops, especially the band saw. I used my money to buy clothing and shoes and sometimes for entertainment.

In the fall of 1949 the Eighth Battalion was dissolved and I was assigned to an arms-training school in Beersheba. There I had the good fortune to pass by a woodworking shop while three brothers deliberated the placement of iron hinges, handles and locks on a very large door. I stood at a distance, observing their discussion and trying to find a solution to the problem myself. Then I approached them and showed them my solution. It worked perfectly. I told them where I was posted and asked if they had a few days' work that I could take on during my free time between courses. They responded in the affirmative. The brothers were very satisfied with my work and gave me assignments whenever I had a free moment. The eldest brother later told me that they were pleased with my work because I never bothered them, found solutions to problems on my own and always finished assignments, regardless of the time of day or how long they took.

Then my mother became very ill with a type of malaria, and I received a transfer to the air base close to Tel Aviv. Army policy was that since I was an only son, I was entitled to compassionate reassignment so that I could be close to my mother. I started out as field security and then took on the management of the office of the airfield commander. I had the responsibility of meeting commanders from different organizations: pilot school, supplies, building, airplane mechanics, car and fleet dispatch, car mechanics, airplane mechanics, kitchen and food, and security and guarding. I had to transmit orders, listen to concerns and then submit them to the commander or his deputy, with suggestions for solutions if possible. I had to use my public relations and diplomacy skills, and I enjoyed the hectic schedule.

Gains and Losses

After being discharged from the army in 1950, I immediately began to look for employment in the building industry. I partnered with a young man who was in the roof, carpentry and framing business. He had learned the trade from his father. He had a motorcycle, and I also purchased and learned how to ride one. I excelled in my role of finding jobs, calculating the quantities of supplies needed, networking with architects and collecting payment for our work. I was working long hours, and our business increased to the point where we sometimes had to hire two to four extra people to finish a job. We had business all over Tel Aviv. However, I was doing the bulk of the work and grew tired of my partner's limitations, and we parted company.

I continued to be busy with assignments, taking on work in new neighbourhoods of three- and four-storey apartment buildings, single homes and high-priced villas, as well as assembling prefabricated homes from Sweden. My days started on-site early in the morning when I prepared and organized the work and sharpened tools, and ended late in the evening after I examined plans and provided tenders and bids for new work. My dream was to become a builder. However, after four years of strenuous physical work I was unable to continue, and I realized that I had to find another vocation. I tried administration at an agricultural journal. The pay was low compared to my previous earnings, and there was no job description; I did whatever was required at the journal: selling advertising, collecting debts, sending the copies out to the regular subscribers. The manager was a good bookkeeper. I asked him if he would teach me bookkeeping in the evenings, and in exchange I did some extra work for him. But unfortunately, I did not find a future for myself in this work.

Like many others my age who came from war-torn Europe, I had no formal education, so decent employment was difficult to obtain. After two or three months I quit the job at the journal and worked full-time with my mother in her dressmaking business. I brought her fabrics and other supplies, delivered the merchandise to stores, cut fabric and generally helped her run the business operations. We rented a store from a builder for whom I had worked. He was originally from the United States and invested with other builders in Israel. After his passing, his sons did not want the burden of maintaining small properties, and they sold us the store. My sister also joined the business, and we hired some seamstresses and other help. I sought out wholesale business, and we sold retail in the store. It was not an easy way to make a living. Many storekeepers did not pay on time, and many failed to pay altogether.

In the summer of 1956 a manufacturer of woollen fabric came to our store and invited me to his warehouse just outside of Tel Aviv, on the road to Jerusalem. He was Russian-born and had come to Israel from Shanghai, where he also had a woollen fabrics factory. He had arrived in Israel just after independence was declared and built a factory that was much bigger than the demands of the Israeli population. He also owned and operated a carpet factory. At his factory he showed me an abundance of fabrics he wanted me to purchase. He told me he wanted to offer the lot to me first to prevent competition from two other dress manufacturers. Based on my knowledge and experience, I knew his price was good. My problem was that I did not have the cash to pay for the lot in full, but the owner asked for a fraction of the full amount up front, with the remainder to be paid later. The lot of fabrics was shipped to us with no issue. I went to visit this man often after this; he always found time to sit and chat with me, and I learned a lot from him. I later discovered that he had selected me as his first contact for the sale of the fabrics because he had heard that I had a reputation of being honest and trustworthy. From this fabric we made patterns for long woollen housecoats, a staple for Israeli winters at the time, as the homes were either not heated or not heated well enough.

When the 1956 Suez Crisis happened, I was immediately mobilized and posted at an infantry unit to command a heavy machine gun platoon. My sister was mobilized to an engineering unit in the Negev. My mother remained with our employees and succeeded in assembling and finishing some housecoats. After several air raid alarms, the demand for our housecoats increased, and our inventory was completely emptied. My mother explained to prospective customers that she could only sell the merchandise for cash payment on the spot, and since we had the only merchandise of this sort, the storekeepers had to comply.

Before we crossed into the Sinai, I envisioned a long drawn-out conflict during which we would be guarding and defending hills and fortifying entrenchments. It was a rather disheartening vision, as I was now thirty years old and had not yet established myself professionally. Before we crossed the Egyptian border, our convoy had to move aside to allow tanks to pass. I started to count the tanks that passed us, and as the number reached over a hundred, I realized that this was going to be very different from the War of Independence.

Our unit was told to prepare for immediate combat. With the stress and the energy-consuming battle ahead of me, I wanted to gather my strength, so I dug myself a little hole and lay down in it to sleep. My comrades could not understand what I was doing and thinking. Many years later, they still asked me how I could have slept under those circumstances, when everybody else in the unit was nervously keeping themselves busy and distracted.

We did not enter combat. Plans changed all the time. We went south with our convoy, using every stop to train and refresh the reserve forces. We then returned to Sarafand, now Tzrifin, south of Tel Aviv, and were discharged, and I returned home.

～

In the late 1940s and early 1950s some family members from Poland discovered us. Two sisters and their husbands — Manya and David, Faya and Shmuel — arrived in Haifa with their children just after Israel's proclamation of independence. They had survived the war by fleeing to Tashkent, in the Soviet Union. Both couples were dedicated to their families and worked hard to support their children and their grandchildren. When they first arrived, Manya and David resided in an old, run-down house in Wadi Rushmia that had been provided by the city of Haifa. With Manya's help, David converted this old house into a cozy home that we enjoyed visiting regularly. They also visited our home after we moved to Ramat Gan. It was crowded in both of our small homes, but we loved the company and did not mind sleeping on mattresses on the floor.

In 1953, the Jewish Agency notified us of the survival of my mother's brother. I believe both of them had registered their details with the Agency as part of their search for family survivors. He arrived in Israel one year later with his new wife and four children. Initially his family lived with us in our small four-hundred-square-foot apartment, and I had to live with friends, changing locations often. He was fifty-five years old, not formally educated and did not speak any Hebrew. He had a very difficult time adjusting to his new circumstances. He was a good shoemaker but too proud, which affected his interactions with people. After he was fired from a few positions because of his arrogance, I found him a store to rent from one of the builders I knew. The store was an immediate success. People brought their shoes for repair and all sorts of work, but the excess work made my uncle nervous and belligerent, and he lost customers and repeat business. After a year it was impossible to maintain the store. He had moved to an apartment in Jaffa, and he needed money to survive. I had to sign his loans, and without telling me, my mother co-signed the same loans. In the end I was left with the responsibility of paying those loans as he became very sick and died of cancer just before his sixtieth birthday.

Just after my army discharge I was required to go to the health office to obtain my health insurance booklet. Upon hearing my last name called, I approached the receptionist at the same time as another young man who also claimed that his name was Schwarzberg. When I asked him where in Poland he came from, he responded that he was from Magnuszew, about sixty kilometres southeast of Warsaw. He was very surprised to learn that I was familiar with this small town and knew that the largest enterprise of its Jewish population before the war was supplying fruit to Warsaw. I called attention to the fact that if he was from Magnuszew there was a strong possibility that we were somehow related. Although I did not know for certain, I knew that my mother would be able to find the connection. He came with me to my mother's apartment, and of course she determined that he was the son of one of her cousins. We even attended his wedding, which was held at a very modest café on Sirkin Street in Tel Aviv.

One day, we received an unexpected visit at the store from a woman, Dina Weintraub, and her daughter, Irka, who were from Poland. They had come to Israel in 1956, arriving with the wave of immigrants who were leaving Poland and Hungary because they opposed their communist rulers. The Weintraubs were looking for employment. My mother realized that they were relatives and hired them without question. Dina had three children, and her husband was being trained to work in the diamond industry, which was a very lucrative business in Israel at that time. We remained friends long after they came to us for help.

My mother became very ill with cancer in the 1950s and had to have surgery twice. The cancer went into remission for a while but returned in 1957, and she was in and out of the hospital. At that time

Dina was no longer working with us but agreed to manage our home and keep my mother company. I travelled with my mother to Jerusalem and to nearly every specialist we were referred to in Tel Aviv and elsewhere in the hope of curing her illness. It was a costly and time-consuming process. I had been told that it was unlikely she would survive the cancer, but I could not bring myself to tell her this. I implored our family doctor, Dr. Schwarz, to visit my mother as often as he could and expressed my readiness to pay for his services. He refused to take any compensation, but he still came to visit my mother whenever he was in the vicinity.

My mother passed away at Tel HaShomer hospital in the spring of 1958. She was only sixty years old, and I was devastated. Her life had been extremely difficult, and she was no stranger to hard work and deprivation. She suffered through both World War II and the Israeli War of Independence with worries for her children and yet never complained. She was the most courageous person I knew.

Epilogue
by Eve Schwarz

My parents met in the late 1950s, after they had both been married briefly to other people. They came to Canada in 1968, after my father fought in the Six-Day War and then spent a year in Germany studying pattern making. They adapted to life in Canada quite quickly, though they were always very Israeli and European in their ways. My parents were extremely frugal — my father never wanted to be indebted to anyone — and they were able to save money, eventually purchasing the two buildings on Richmond Street where his garment factory and warehouse were, and then several other investment properties and a condo in Israel.

My father's sister, Lea, remained in Israel and had two children, Ayal and Odine, and she and my father had a close relationship throughout the years. Lea spent several summers in Toronto, and my parents spent time with her when they were in Israel for winters.

As far back as I can remember, my father told his war stories to me and to whomever was interested. I believe that his stories are branded into his soul, an essential part of him. Eventually, when he retired after twenty-five years in the garment industry and became less active, he found a way to share his experiences and find emotional release by writing down his stories. As he finished each chapter of this book, he would give me the material to review and edit.

My father often talks about how he was saved several times by strangers — people who showed him the way, provided him with food or lodging, with fake papers or with other big and small acts of kindness. He believes that without these helpers, he would not be here and would not have enjoyed such a long life. To me, the message that my father's memoir imparts is a universal one: the world, a country, a community or neighbourhood can be subject to a malevolent power, yet even under such circumstances, there are always the helpers, the humanitarians, the ones that will risk their lives to make things better. My father, along with many others, was one of those.

Glossary

aliyah (Hebrew; pl. *aliyot*, literally, ascent) A term used by Jews and modern Israelis to refer to Jewish immigration to Israel; the term is also used to refer to "going up" to the altar in a synagogue to read from the Torah.

Allied forces (Allies) The coalition of countries that fought against Germany, Italy and Japan (the Axis nations). At the beginning of World War II, in September 1939, the coalition included France, Poland and Britain. Once Germany invaded the USSR in June 1941 and the United States entered the war following the bombing of Pearl Harbor by Japan on December 7, 1941, the main leaders of the Allied powers became Britain, the USSR and the United States. Other Allies included Canada, Australia, Czechoslovakia, Greece, Mexico, Brazil, South Africa and China.

Amitié Chrétienne (French; Christian Friendship/Fellowship) An organization founded by L'Abbé Alexandre Glasberg in 1940 that established shelters for Jewish and non-Jewish refugees who were persecuted by the Nazis. *See also* Glasberg, Alexandre.

antisemitism Prejudice, discrimination, persecution or hatred against Jewish people, institutions, culture and symbols.

Arab Legion A police force formed by the British in 1923 to protect the Transjordan region. In the 1930s the Arab Legion became known as the most effective and well-trained Arab army. They withdrew from Palestine with the British prior to the end of the British Mandate and then invaded the newly declared State of Israel with other Arab armies on May 15, 1948. In the 1950s the Legion was renamed the Jordanian Armed Forces, and it is also known as the Arab Army.

Arbeitseinsatz (German; labour deployment) Unpaid labour, often under brutal conditions, that the Nazis forced millions of Jews and non-Jews to perform. In some cases, Jewish men and women were taken out of the ghettos each day and returned at night; in other cases, they were transported to forced labour camps in other regions or countries.

Ardennes Offensive Also known as the Battle of the Bulge. The German counteroffensive in the Ardennes region of Belgium and Luxembourg that began on December 16, 1944. Germany's plan was to capture Antwerp and encircle and destroy the Allied armies. Initially successful, it created a huge "bulge" in the American line of advance but was stopped well short of its objective — Antwerp. By January 28, 1945, the Germans had been forced back to their original positions. The battle resulted in over 90,000 Allied casualties, 3,000 of which were civilian deaths.

Armée secrète (AS) (French; secret army) A French resistance movement created from three separate resistance groups that supported Charles de Gaulle. They joined together in September 1942 in order to more effectively fight the Nazi occupiers of France. *See also* de Gaulle, Charles; French Resistance.

Army of Africa The French army stationed in French North Africa. During World War II the army first fought for Vichy France and then merged with Charles de Gaulle's Free French Forces in 1943 to fight alongside the Allies, taking part in the invasion of Southern France after the invasion of Normandy in 1944. *See also* Free French Forces; Vichy.

Aryanization The process of transferring businesses owned by Jews to non-Jews in Germany and countries occupied by Germany during the 1930s and World War II. This was done initially through limits placed on Jewish involvement in the economy and later through confiscation of businesses.

Auschwitz (German; in Polish, Oświęcim) A town in southern Poland approximately forty kilometres from Krakow, it is also the name of the largest complex of Nazi concentration camps that were built nearby. The Auschwitz complex contained three main camps: Auschwitz I, a slave labour camp built in May 1940; Auschwitz II-Birkenau, a death camp built in early 1942; and Auschwitz-Monowitz, a slave labour camp built in October 1942. In 1941, Auschwitz I was a testing site for usage of the lethal gas Zyklon B as a method of mass killing, which then went into wide usage. Between 1942 and 1944, transports arrived at Auschwitz-Birkenau from almost every country in Europe — hundreds of thousands from both Poland and Hungary, and thousands from France, the Netherlands, Greece, Slovakia, Bohemia and Moravia, Yugoslavia, Belgium, Italy and Norway. As well, more than 30,000 people were deported there from other concentration camps. It is estimated that 1.1 million people were murdered in Auschwitz; approximately 950,000 were Jewish; 74,000 Polish; 21,000 Roma; 15,000 Soviet prisoners of war; and 10,000–15,000 other nationalities. The Auschwitz complex was liberated by the Soviet army in January 1945.

Bar Lev, Chaim (1924–1994) An Israeli war hero, military officer and politician. Born Chaim Brotzlewsky in Austria, Bar-Lev moved to British Mandate Palestine in 1939, where he fought for the Palmach and became a commander and then chief of staff of the Israeli army (1968–1972). Bar-Lev was a member of the Knesset (parliament), a minister of Trade and Industry, secretary general of the Labour Party and ambassador to Moscow. *See also* Palmach.

bar mitzvah (Hebrew; literally, son of the commandment) The time when, in Jewish tradition, children become religiously and morally responsible for their actions and are considered adults for the purpose of synagogue and other rituals. Traditionally this occurs at age thirteen for boys and twelve for girls. A bar mitzvah is also the synagogue ceremony and family celebration that mark the attainment of this status, during which the boy is called upon to read a portion of the Torah and recite the prescribed prayers in a public prayer service. In the latter half of the twentieth century, liberal Jews instituted an equivalent ceremony and celebration for girls called a bat mitzvah. Variations of this ceremony for girls are often held in Orthodox practice as well.

Bedouin Nomadic Arabs who dwell in Middle Eastern and North African desert regions.

black market An illegal and informal economic system that arises, often in wartime, due to shortages or government control of goods.

British Mandate Palestine The area of the Middle East under British rule from 1923 to 1948, as established by the League of Nations after World War I. During that time, the United Kingdom severely restricted Jewish immigration. The Mandate area encompassed present-day Israel, Jordan, the West Bank and the Gaza Strip.

Burg, Dr. Yosef (1909–1999) A German-born rabbi and academic who became an Israeli politician. Burg received a doctorate in philosophy in 1933 and rabbinical ordination in 1938. Before the war, he was active in a Zionist youth movement and helped Jews escape from Germany. In 1939 he immigrated to British Mandate Palestine, where he joined the religious Zionist political party Hapoel HaMizrachi. In 1949 he was elected to the Knesset (parliament), serving until 1988. Burg cofounded the National Religious Party in 1956, served in a variety of ministerial positions in the Israeli government and was known for his efforts to heal rifts between religious and secular Israelis.

Camp Vernet (also Le Vernet D'Ariège) A concentration camp in the Ariège Département of France, near Toulouse. In 1939 the French army began using the site to intern refugees, political extremists and people deemed to be German sympathizers. In 1940, after the signing of the armistice between France and Germany, the Vichy government took over Le Vernet and it became a men's work camp that dealt harshly with leftists and foreigners considered dangerous to the government. In 1942 and 1944, Vernet served as a holding camp for Jews who were being sent to Dachau and other concentration camps. Some Jews remained in the camp, where they were singled out for harsh treatment. After the Germans occupied the south of France in 1942, they became involved in running the camp and took over its administration in June 1944, sending most of the remaining inmates to Dachau. The camp was liberated on August 23, 1944, and was then turned into a P O W camp for Germans. *See also* Dachau; Vichy.

Carlebach School The Orthodox Jewish school founded in Germany in 1912 by Ephraim Carlebach, of the prominent German rabbinic Carlebach family.

Château du Bégué An agricultural reception centre in Cazaubon, in the Vichy-controlled southern zone of France, that was founded by Alexandre Glasberg and managed by Vila Glasberg to save Jews and political refugees who were hiding from the Nazis. The centre, which was owned by Count and Countess Henri and Simone d'André, housed more than a hundred residents who did agricultural labour and became involved in underground resistance activities. *See also* d'André, Henri; Glasberg, Alexandre; Vermont, Victor.

Dachau The Nazis' first concentration camp, which was established primarily to house political prisoners in March 1933. The Dachau camp was located about sixteen kilometres northwest of Munich in southern Germany. The number of Jews interned there rose considerably after Kristallnacht pogroms on the night of November 9–10, 1938. In 1942 a crematorium area was constructed next to the main camp. By the spring of 1945, Dachau and its subcamps held more than 67,665 registered prisoners — 43,350 categorized as political prisoners and 22,100 as Jews. As the American Allied forces neared the camp in April 1945, the Nazis forced 7,000 prisoners, primarily Jews, on a gruelling death march to Tegernsee, another camp in southern Germany.

d'André, Henri (1897–1974) A French count who, with his wife, Countess Simone d'André (1907–1983), made their property — Château du Bégué in Cazaubon — available to Amitié Chrétienne and the Glasberg brothers to organize a place of refuge for more than a hundred Jews and political refugees. They were named Righteous Among the Nations in November 2006. *See also* Amitié Chrétienne; Glasberg, Alexandre; Righteous Among the Nations; Vermont, Victor.

Débarquement See Normandy landings.

de Gaulle, Charles André Joseph Marie (1890–1970) A French general and statesman who opposed both the Nazi regime and the French collaborationist Vichy government. De Gaulle, a World War I veteran and Brigadier General in World War II, escaped to London after the fall of France in 1940. In London, de Gaulle organized the Free French Forces, a partisan and resistance group comprised of French officers in exile. After the war, de Gaulle served as head of the French provisional government from 1944 to 1946, and as president of France from 1958 to 1969. *See also* Free French Forces; Vichy.

Drancy A northeastern suburb of Paris that was the site of an internment and transit camp from which about 65,000 people, almost all Jews, were deported to concentration and death camps. Established in August 1941, the camp was run by the French police until July 1943, when it was taken over by the Nazi SS. Drancy was liberated in August 1944.

Feldgendarmerie (singular, *Feldgendarme*; plural, *Feldgendarmes*) Military police units of the German armed forces that were active in World War I, disbanded after the war and were reintroduced by Nazi Germany. *Feldgendarmerie* units were usually active in German-occupied territories where they worked closely with the SS and were known for their brutal disciplining of German soldiers who were deserters or otherwise violated military law. *See also* SS.

fifth column A group of people who are clandestinely collaborating with an invading enemy. The term was first used by the Nationalists in the Spanish Civil War of 1936–1939 to refer to their supporters within the territories controlled by the Republican side. Because these people were helping the four columns of the Nationalists' army, they were deemed to be their "fifth column."

Forces Françaises de l'Intérieur (French Forces of the Interior, FFI) The movement created in early 1944 that unified the existing resistance groups in occupied France. In effect, many of the groups still maintained their autonomy. After the liberation of Paris in August 1944, the FFI was integrated into the French army by Charles de Gaulle. *See also* de Gaulle, Charles; French Resistance.

Franco, Francisco (1892–1975) A Spanish general and dictator who was the head of state of Spain from 1939 to 1975. Franco, who led the Nationalists in victory against the Republicans in the Spanish Civil War, at first remained officially neutral and then "non-belligerent" during World War II, but lent military support to the Axis powers. Paradoxically, his authoritarian, fascist regime did not follow an antisemitic policy of interning Jews unless they were stateless, instead allowing approximately 30,000 Jewish refugees who had documentation into Spain, often on their way through to neutral Portugal. *See also* Spanish Civil War.

Francs-Tireurs et Partisans (FTP) (French; Partisan Irregular Riflemen) The French resistance group that was the military branch of the French Communist Party. They became active in 1941, ambushing and killing occupying German soldiers and carrying out missions to sabotage rail lines and factories working for the German war effort. *See also* French Resistance; *Maquis*.

Free French Forces A military force comprising partisan and resistance groups of French officers in exile led by Charles de Gaulle during World War II. After the Nazi occupation of France, the forces continued to fight against the German military. De Gaulle led both the Free French Forces and the Provisional Government of the French Republic, an interim government that ruled from 1944 to 1946. *See also* de Gaulle, Charles.

French Communist Party (in French, Parti communiste français; PCF) A political party founded on communist principles in 1920. The party was led by Maurice Thorez in 1930 and supported the Popular Front government of 1936. When Germany invaded the Soviet Union in June 1941, the party engaged in armed resistance against the German occupiers, setting up a resistance group called Francs-Tireurs et Partisans (FTP). *See also* Francs-Tireurs et Partisans.

French Foreign Legion (FFL) A branch of the French army that was established in 1831 to bypass the restriction of foreigners serving in the French armed forces, allowing foreign nationals to serve in the military. The legion's headquarters were in Algeria and during the nineteenth century its members primarily fought to expand the French empire. During World War II, legionnaires served in Norway, Syria and North Africa. Currently, the Legion's headquarters are in Aubagne, France.

French Resistance The collective term for the French resistance movement during World War II. In rural areas, the group was known as the *Maquis*. The Resistance published underground newspapers, helped Allied prisoners-of-war escape, sabotaged German war equipment and created intelligence networks that gathered military information in order to gain armament support from Britain. *See also Maquis*.

gendarmes Members of a military or paramilitary force, a gendarmerie.

Geneva Conventions A set of treaties and protocols that were negotiated between 1864 and 1949 to establish an international law for the standards of humanitarian treatment of victims of war, both military and civilian.

Gestapo (German; abbreviation of Geheime Staatspolizei, the Secret State Police of Nazi Germany) The Gestapo were the brutal force that dealt with the perceived enemies of the Nazi regime and were responsible for rounding up European Jews for deportation to the death camps. They operated with very few legal constraints and were also responsible for issuing exit visas to the residents of German-occupied areas. A number of Gestapo members also joined the Einsatzgruppen, the mobile killing squads responsible for the roundup and murder of Jews in eastern Poland and the USSR through mass shooting operations.

Glasberg, (Abbé) Alexandre (1902–1981) A Ukrainian-born Jew who converted to Catholicism, was ordained a priest in 1938 and became a vicar in the suburbs of Lyon, where he carried out rescue and resistance activities with his brother, Vila (Victor Vermont). In 1940 he founded Amitié Chrétienne to assist Jews and political refugees hiding from the Nazis. Post-war, Glasberg was involved in helping Jews emigrate from Europe and from Arab countries to Israel. He was recognized as Righteous Among the Nations in 2003. *See also* Amitié Chrétienne; Righteous Among the Nations; Vermont, Victor.

Glasberg, Vila See Vermont, Victor.

Habima Theatre Israel's national theatre, established in Białystok (then part of the Russian Empire) in 1912 as a Hebrew language theatre focusing on Jewish stories and themes. The theatre relocated to British Mandate Palestine in 1931 and is located in central Tel Aviv.

hachshara (Hebrew; literally, preparation) A training program to prepare new immigrants for life in the Land of Israel.

Haganah (Hebrew; Defence) The Jewish paramilitary force in British Mandate Palestine that existed from 1920 to 1948 and later became the Israel Defense Forces. After World War II, there were branches of the Haganah in the DP camps in Europe, and members helped coordinate illegal immigration to British Mandate Palestine. *See also* Palmach.

Hashomer Hatzair (Hebrew) The Youth Guard. A left-wing Zionist youth movement founded in Central Europe in the early twentieth century to prepare young Jews to become workers and farmers, to establish kibbutzim — collective settlements — in pre-state Israel and work the land as pioneers. Before World War II, there were 70,000 Hashomer Hatzair members worldwide and many of those in Nazi-occupied territories led resistance activities in the ghettos and concentration camps or joined partisan groups in the forests of east-central Europe. It is the oldest Zionist youth movement still in existence. *See also* Zionism.

Hauptsturmführer (German; head storm leader) A Nazi paramilitary rank equivalent to that of captain.

heliograph A signalling device that uses the reflection of sunlight off mirrors to communicate.

Histadrut (Hebrew; abbreviation of HaHistadrut HaKlalit shel Ha-Ovdim B'Eretz Yisrael; General Federation of Labourers in the Land of Israel) A labour union established in pre-state Israel in 1920. A branch was established in Montreal in 1943.

humanism A philosophy developed in the Renaissance that emphasizes the dignity of every human being and a rational approach to the fulfillment of human needs and potential.

International Brigades The general name for the military units that volunteered from more than fifty countries to support the Spanish Republic by fighting against the fascist Nationalist forces during the Spanish Civil War. Between 40,000 and 60,000 volunteers held either combative or non-combative roles between 1936 and 1939. *See also* Spanish Civil War.

Jewish Agency for Israel (in Hebrew, Sochnut) The organization established by the World Zionist Organization in 1929 that was largely responsible for the economic and cultural development of pre-state Israel, as well as the immigration and resettlement of Jews from the Diaspora in British Mandate Palestine and later Israel. With the Nazi Party's rise to power, the Sochnut advocated for increasing the legal quota of immigrants to Palestine and helped establish the Youth Aliyah program to help children escape Nazi Europe. The Sochnut currently focuses on strengthening Jewish identity in Israel and worldwide. *See also* aliyah; Youth Aliyah.

Jewish Brigade A battalion that was formed in September 1944 under the command of the British Eighth Army. The Jewish Brigade included more than 5,000 volunteers from Palestine. After the war, the Brigade was essential in helping Jewish refugees and organizing their entry into Palestine. It was disbanded by the British in 1946.

kangaroo court An impromptu and unofficial court that is held to try people who are seen as having committed a crime, often condemning people without evidence and rendering unjust verdicts.

kibbutz (Hebrew) A collectively owned farm or settlement in Israel, democratically governed by its members.

Kristallnacht (German; literally, Night of Broken Glass) A series of pogroms that took place in Germany and Austria between November 9 and 10, 1938. Over the course of twenty-four hours, ninety-one Jews were murdered, 25,000–30,000 were arrested and deported to concentration camps, two hundred synagogues were destroyed and thousands of Jewish businesses and homes were ransacked. Planned by the Nazis as a coordinated attack on the Jews of Germany and Austria, Kristallnacht is often seen as an important turning point in Hitler's policies of systematic persecution of Jews.

laissez-passer (French; let pass) A travel document issued by a government or international organization to people who are stateless or unable to obtain a passport, often used in wartime to allow travel to specific destinations.

Laval, Pierre Jean-Marie (1883–1945) A French politician who served as prime minister of France from January 1931 to February 1932 and again from June 1935 to January 1936. Laval also headed the Vichy government between April 1942 and August 1944. A rightwing collaborator, Laval went beyond compliance with German requests to actively seek out foreign-born Jewish children for deportation from France. He was tried for treason after the war ended and was executed by firing squad.

League of Nations An international organization of countries created after World War I to resolve international disputes and prevent war. It was replaced by the United Nations in 1945. *See also* United Nations.

Les Compagnons de France (French; The Companions of France) A French youth organization for boys between the ages of fifteen and twenty, founded in June 1940. Initially supported by the Vichy government, the organization promoted physical activity and national service, such as assisting with farm work. The movement was dissolved by the Germans in 1944.

Maquis (French; derived from the word *maquisards*; thicket) The term for French resistance fighters in rural areas during World War II. The *Maquis* originated from a group of men, mostly communist and socialist, who fled to mountainous terrain (hence their name, which loosely translates as "bush") to avoid being arrested by the Gestapo in occupied France due to their political orientation. By early 1943, the *Maquis* had grown in strength and organization due to the thousands of new members who were avoiding the new law of conscription in France, the Service du Travail Obligatoire, which led to forced labour in Germany. The *Maquis* at first focused on sabotaging German communication and transport lines as well as providing protection to Jews and refugees, and later were able to organize armed resistance due to British and American support. After the Normandy landings on June 6, 1944, the *Maquis* became formalized into the French Forces of the Interior. *See also* French Resistance.

Molotov-Ribbentrop Pact Also known as the Treaty of Non-Aggression between Germany and the USSR. The treaty that was signed on August 24, 1939, by Soviet foreign minister Vyacheslav Molotov and German foreign minister Joachim von Ribbentrop. The main provisions of the pact stipulated that the two countries would not go to war with each other and that they would both remain neutral if either one was attacked by a third party. One of the key components of the treaty was the division of various independent countries — including Poland — into Nazi and Soviet spheres of influence and areas of occupation. The Nazis breached the pact by launching a major offensive against the Soviet Union on June 22, 1941.

moshav (Hebrew; literally, settlement or village) An agricultural cooperative comprised of individually owned farms that was founded by the Labour Zionist movement in the early twentieth century.

Nansen passport An identity card issued to stateless refugees by the League of Nations High Commission for Refugees, named after its designer, the Norwegian explorer, scientist and diplomat Fridtjof Nansen. The passport was created in 1922 and by 1942 was honoured by fifty-two countries. It was the first travel document for stateless refugees, and in 1938 the Nansen International Office for Refugees was awarded the Nobel Peace Prize for its pioneering work.

Normandy landings Also referred to as D-Day. The Allied invasion of Normandy, France, on June 6, 1944, that marked the onset of the liberation of Western Europe during World War II. Nearly 150,000 Allied troops arrived by boat or parachute to participate in this invasion.

Nuremberg Laws The September 1935 laws that stripped Jews of their civil rights as German citizens and separated them from Germans legally, socially and politically. They were first announced at the Nazi Party rally in the city of Nuremberg in 1933. Under "The Law for the Protection of German Blood and Honour," Jews were defined as a separate race rather than a religious group; whether a person was racially Jewish was determined by ancestry (how many Jewish grandparents a person had). Among other things, the law forbade marriages or sexual relations between Jews and Germans.

Oberfeldwebel (German; senior sergeant) A non-commissioned officer (NCO) rank in the German army and air force that is equivalent to sergeant.

Orthodox Judaism The set of beliefs and practices of Jews for whom the observance of Jewish law is closely connected to faith; it is characterized by strict religious observance of Jewish dietary laws, restrictions on work on the Sabbath and holidays, and a code of modesty in dress.

Palais de Justice (French; The Palace of Justice) A vast complex of law courts in Brussels built between 1866 and 1883.

Palmach (Hebrew acronym for Plugot Machatz; literally, strike forces) A military brigade in British Mandate Palestine that was established in 1941 and initially served as a support for the British Army. In the fall of 1942, the British Army ordered the Palmach to be disbanded and it instead went underground, becoming an independent defence force until the modern state of Israel was founded in 1948.

Pétain, Philippe (1856–1951) A French general and Maréchal (Marshal) of France who was the chief of state of the French government in Vichy from 1940 to 1944. After the war Pétain was tried for treason for his collaboration with the Nazis and sentenced to death, which was commuted to life imprisonment. *See also* Vichy.

Reform Judaism Also known as Progressive Judaism, Reform Judaism emerged in nineteenth-century Germany in response to the previous century's rise in secularism in Europe, the Haskalah

(Jewish Enlightenment) and Jewish emancipation, which allowed Jews more social and economic freedom. The Reform movement introduced a variety of changes in Jewish observance, including incorporating the local language into religious services in place of, or in addition to, Hebrew.

Righteous Among the Nations A title bestowed by Yad Vashem, the Holocaust Martyrs' and Heroes' Remembrance Authority in Jerusalem, to honour non-Jews who risked their lives to help save Jews during the Holocaust. A commission was established in 1963 to award the title. If a person fits certain criteria and the story is carefully corroborated, the honouree is awarded with a medal and certificate and commemorated on the Wall of Honour at the Garden of the Righteous in Jerusalem. *See also* Yad Vashem.

Russian Revolution The 1917 February and October revolutions that led to the dissolution of the autocratic tsarist regime and the creation of a communist government, respectively. The provisional government established after the February revolt was defeated by the Bolsheviks in October. The Bolshevik government — also referred to as the "reds" — was subsequently challenged by the "whites" or anti-Bolsheviks, which resulted in a five-year civil war.

SA (abbreviation of Sturmabteilung; assault division, usually translated as "storm troopers") The SA served as the paramilitary wing of the Nazi Party and played a key role in Hitler's rise to power in the 1930s. Members of the SA were often called "Brown Shirts" for the colour of their uniforms, which distinguished them from Heinrich Himmler's all-black SS (Schutzstaffel) uniforms. The SA was effectively superseded by the SS after the 1934 purge within the Nazi party known as the "Night of the Long Knives." *See also* SS.

Sachsenhausen A concentration camp located north of Berlin, Germany, established in 1936. Its first inmates were homosexuals, Roma, political prisoners, Jehovah's Witnesses and Jews. With the onset of the war, the camp began to hold Polish and Czech prisoners, as well as Soviet POWs, and in 1942 most of the Jews were sent to Auschwitz. In the early years of the camp, prisoners were put to work building the camp and nearby facilities, but once the war started they began manufacturing military equipment for the war effort. Inmates of the camp were in constant danger of being tortured and killed at random, and the camp contained a killing facility that housed a gas chamber and crematorium. By January 1945, Sachsenhausen and its subcamps contained around 70,000 prisoners, but there were only about 3,000 remaining in the camp when the Soviets liberated it on April 22 of that year. Estimates put the total deaths at Sachsenhausen at 40,000–50,000.

SD (abbreviation of Sicherheitsdienst, the security and intelligence service of the SS) The main responsibility of the SD, which was headed by Reinhard Heydrich under the command of Heinrich Himmler, was to seek out supposed enemies of the Third Reich through huge networks of informants in the occupied territories. *See also* SS.

Shabbat (Hebrew; in Yiddish, Shabbes, Shabbos) The weekly day of rest beginning Friday at sunset and ending Saturday at nightfall, ushered in by the lighting of candles on Friday evening and the recitation of blessings over wine and challah (egg bread). A day of celebration as well as prayer, it is customary to eat three festive meals, attend synagogue services and refrain from doing any work or travelling.

Sharon, Ariel (1928–2014) An officer in the Israeli army who moved into politics and served as prime minister of Israel from March 2001 to April 2006.

Spanish Civil War (1936–1939) The war in Spain between the military — supported by Conservative, Catholic and fascist elements, together called the Nationalists — and the Republican government. Sparked by an initial coup that failed to win a decisive victory, the country was plunged into a bloody civil war. It ended when the Nationalists, under the leadership of General Francisco

Franco, marched into Madrid. During the civil war, the Nationalists received aid from both Fascist Italy and Nazi Germany, and
the Republicans received aid from volunteers worldwide. *See also*
Franco, Francisco; International Brigades.

SS (abbreviation of Schutzstaffel; Defence Corps) The SS was established in 1925 as Adolf Hitler's elite corps of personal bodyguards.
Under the direction of Heinrich Himmler, its membership grew
from 280 in 1929 to 50,000 when the Nazis came to power in 1933,
and to nearly a quarter of a million on the eve of World War II.
The SS was comprised of the Allgemeine-SS (General SS) and the
Waffen-SS (Armed, or Combat SS). The General SS dealt with
policing and the enforcement of Nazi racial policies in Germany
and the Nazi-occupied countries. An important unit within the
SS was the Reichssicherheitshauptamt (RSHA, the Central Office of Reich Security), whose responsibility included the Gestapo
(Geheime Staatspolizei). The SS ran the concentration and death
camps, with all their associated economic enterprises, and also
fielded its own Waffen-SS military divisions, including some recruited from the occupied countries. *See also* Gestapo.

Stalin, Joseph (1878–1953) The leader of the Soviet Union from 1924
until his death in 1953. Born Joseph Vissarionovich Dzhugashvili,
he changed his name to Stalin (literally, man of steel) in 1903. Very
soon after acquiring leadership of the Communist Party, Stalin
ousted rivals, killed opponents in purges, and effectively established himself as a dictator. During the late 1930s, Stalin com-
menced "The Great Purge," during which he targeted and dis-
posed of elements within the Communist Party that he deemed
to be a threat to the stability of the Soviet Union. These purges
extended to both military and civilian society, and millions of
people were incarcerated or exiled to harsh labour camps.

Star of David (in Hebrew, *Magen David*) The six-pointed star that
is the ancient and most recognizable symbol of Judaism. During
World War II, Jews in Nazi-occupied areas were frequently forced

to wear a badge or armband with the Star of David on it as an identifying mark of their lesser status and to single them out as targets for persecution.

Steg, Ady (born Adolphe; 1925–) A well-known Czech-born professor of medicine. During the war, Ady, his brother, Henry, and his sister, Albertine, were living in Paris and were rescued by Abbé Glasberg and sheltered at Château du Bégué, Cazaubon. After the war, Steg studied medicine and became a professor and surgeon, serving as a doctor to both General de Gaulle and President François Mitterand. Steg has held leadership positions within several French Jewish organizations, including Le Conseil représentatif des institutions juives de France (Representative Council of Jewish Institutions in France, CRIF), L' Alliance israélite universelle (The Universal Israelite Alliance) and the Foundation for the Memory of the Holocaust. *See also* Château du Bégué; Glasberg, Abbé.

Sturmbannführer (German; storm unit leader) A Nazi paramilitary rank equivalent to that of major.

Suez Crisis Also known as the Tripartite Aggression, Sinai War and the Second Arab-Israeli War. The October and November 1956 conflict between Egypt and Israel, France and Britain over the ownership of the Suez Canal, an essential route for oil shipments. Mediated by the first-ever United Nations Emergency Force, the conflict ended with Israel's withdrawal of troops in March 1957.

Talmud Torah (Hebrew; study of Torah) A community-supported Jewish elementary school that provided a basic education in Torah and the Hebrew language to orphans and children from impoverished families. Talmud Torah schools today are tuition-based.

Trotsky, Leon (born Lev Davidovich Bronstein, 1879–1940) A Russian revolutionary, leader of the Red Army and Soviet politician. Trotsky played a major role in the Russian Revolution and developed his own version of Marxism, Trotskyism, that supported worldwide revolution and was critical of the bureaucracy that developed under Stalin. Trotsky served as leader of the anti-Stalin opposition but was expelled from the Communist Party in 1927 and exiled from the Soviet Union in 1929. He was assassinated by a Stalinist agent in Mexico in 1940. *See also* Russian Revolution; Stalin, Joseph.

Union de la jeunesse juive (French; Union of Jewish Youth, UJJ) A youth organization established in 1943 that was led by communists from the Jewish section of the Main-d'œuvre immigrée. It was active mainly in Lyon and Grenoble. The UJJ merged in 1945 with the Union de la jeunesse républicaine de France.

United Nations (UN) A global organization that replaced the League of Nations after World War II in order to prevent further international conflict, to confront challenges affecting the international community and to promote international cooperation and welfare. The UN started with 51 member states and has grown to include 193 member states. *See also* League of Nations.

United Nations Partition Plan for Palestine The United Nations' recommendation for the division of post-British Mandate Palestine into independent Arab and Jewish states with Jerusalem under international control. The plan was adopted on November 29, 1947, by the UN General Assembly. It was accepted by the Jewish Agency for Israel and rejected by Arab leaders, and fighting broke out immediately after the resolution was passed. *See also* British Mandate Palestine; United Nations.

V Day (Victory Day) The holiday that commemorates victory in war in a country's history.

Vermont, Victor (alias for Vila Glasberg; 1907–1944) The brother of Abbé Alexandre Glasberg, whom Vermont assisted in rescuing Jews in France during World War II. Vermont was the manager of the Château du Bégué in Cazaubon until he was arrested by the Gestapo in August 1943; he was deported and murdered in Auschwitz in March 1944. *See also* Château du Bégué; Glasberg, Alexandre.

Vichy A resort town in south-central France that was the seat of the government of Maréchal Pétain in unoccupied France. The Franco-German armistice of June 22, 1940, divided France into two zones: the northern three-fifths to be under German military occupation and the remaining southern region to be under nominal French sovereignty, also referred to as the *zone libre* (free zone). In October 1940 the administration in Vichy enacted antisemitic legislation, independently of Germany, and later collaborated with Nazi Germany by interning Jews in Drancy, which later led to their deportation to death camps. *See also* Drancy; Pétain, Philippe.

War of Independence Also known as the 1948 Arab-Israeli War or the first Arab-Israeli War. The conflict between the state of Israel and Arab forces after Israel's independence was declared on May 14, 1948.

Yad Vashem The Holocaust Martyrs' and Heroes' Remembrance Authority, established in 1953 to commemorate, educate the public about, research and document the Holocaust.

Yom Kippur (Hebrew; Day of Atonement) A solemn day of fasting and repentance that comes eight days after Rosh Hashanah, the Jewish New Year, and marks the end of the High Holidays.

Zionism A movement promoted by the Viennese Jewish journalist Theodor Herzl, who argued in his 1896 book *Der Judenstaat* (The Jewish State) that the best way to resolve the problem of antisemitism and persecution of Jews in Europe was to create an independent Jewish state in the historic Jewish homeland of Biblical Israel. Zionists also promoted the revival of Hebrew as a Jewish national language.

zone libre (French; free zone) The southern region of France that was under nominal French sovereignty between June 1940 and November 1942, after which it was occupied by Germany. *See also* Vichy.

Photographs

1 Joseph's maternal grandmother. Poland, date unknown.
2 Joseph's mother, Chava (Eva) Schwarzberg, with one of her brothers. Warsaw, Poland, 1920s.
3 Joseph's father, Noach (Natan) Swieczka. Poland, date unknown.
4 Joseph's father, Noach (left), with his brother. Poland, date unknown.

1   2

3

1 Joseph at age six in his school uniform. Leipzig, Germany, 1932.
2 Joseph with his mother, Chava Schwarzberg, and his father, Noach Swieczka.
   Leipzig, Germany, 1932.
3 Joseph and his sister, Lea. Leipzig, Germany, circa 1933.

1

2

1 Joseph's class in the Jewish school. Joseph is in the second row, third from the left.
   Leipzig, Germany, circa 1933.

2 Joseph's parents with their friends the Tomarkins. Joseph's father, Noach, is in the
   front row, second from the left, and his mother, Chava, is in the back row, fifth
   from the left. Leipzig, Germany, circa 1936.

Joseph with his mother, Chava, and his sister, Lea. Leipzig, Germany, circa 1938.

1 Joseph. Brussels, Belgium, 1940.

2 Joseph. Brussels, Belgium, circa 1942.

3 Joseph with his friends from school in Leipzig. From left to right: Harry Grunbaum, Manny Hausman, Joseph. Brussels, Belgium, 1940.

4 Joseph with his mother, Chava, and his sister, Lea. Brussels, Belgium, circa 1942.

1

2

3

1 The agricultural school at the Château du Bégué where Joseph lived for about a
  year. From left to right: two residents of the château, names unknown; Joseph's
  friends Ady and Henry Steg; Joseph. Cazaubon, France, circa 1942.

2 Joseph (right) with his friends Ady (left) and Albertine (centre) Steg at Château
  du Bégué. Cazaubon, France, circa 1942.

3 A letter confirming that Joseph — under his alias, Joseph Sarlat — is employed at
  the Agricultural Centre in Cazaubon. 1943. Courtesy of Yad Vashem.

Joseph's forged identity card, issued in Lyon on April 12, 1943, in the name of Joseph Jean Sarlat, born in Amiens, France, June 17, 1926. Courtesy of Yad Vashem.

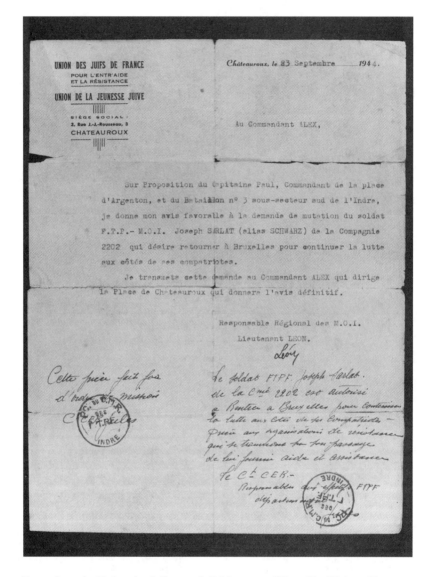

Letter from the Union des Juifs pour la Résistance et l'Entraide (Union of Jews for Resistance and Mutual Aid [UJRE]) in Châteauroux regarding the transfer of Joseph Sarlat (a Francs-Tireurs et Partisans — Main-D'œuvre Immigrée [FTP-MOI] soldier) to Belgium, dated September 23, 1944, and signed by Lieutenant Léon. The handwritten note stipulates that Joseph Sarlat be given whatever help he needs on his way to Brussels. Courtesy of Yad Vashem.

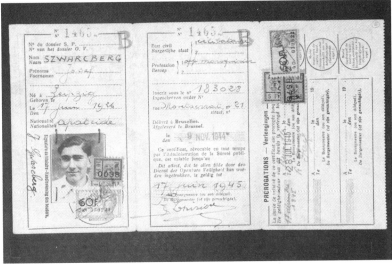

1 One of the photos of the victory parade in Châteauroux that Joseph purchased
   shortly after he participated in it. Châteauroux, France, September 1944.

2 Registration certificate for foreign residents issued in Brussels on November 9,
   1944, to Josef Szwarcberg, born in Leipzig, Germany, June 17, 1926. Courtesy of
   Yad Vashem.

Joseph's mother, Chava, after the war. Date and place unknown.

1 & 2   A questionnaire from the Palestine Office completed on August 10, 1945, by Joseph Schwarzberg and stamped by the Government of Palestine, Department of Migration on his entry into Palestine, September 8, 1945. Courtesy of Yad Vashem.

3   Joseph's troops in the Negev. Palestine, circa 1947.

1 & 2 Joseph building fortifications during his army service in the Negev. Palestine,
1947.

3 Joseph leading his troops. Palestine, circa 1947.

1

2

1 Joseph with his troops in the mountains at the Egyptian border. Israel, circa 1948.
2 Joseph (left) in Ma'aleh Akrabim. Israel, circa 1948.

1 Joseph and his wife, Schulamit, with their daughter, Eve. Israel, circa 1967.
2 From left to right: Joseph's niece, Odine; his nephew, Ayal; his daughter, Eve; his sister, Lea; and his wife, Schulamit. Canada, circa 1972.

Joseph and his wife, Schulamit, featured in an article about their garment business, Adina J. Fashions. Toronto, circa 1980s.

1 Joseph's seventieth birthday celebration. From left to right: Joseph's sister, Lea; his wife, Schulamit; Joseph. Toronto, 1996.

2 Joseph and his wife, Schulamit. Toronto, 2002.

1

2

1 Joseph at his daughter Eve's wedding. From left to right: Eve's husband, Rob; Eve; Joseph; Joseph's wife, Schulamit; Joseph's grandson, Austin Knights; and Austin's wife, Tereiss Oliver. Toronto, 2015.

2 On the boardwalk at The Beaches in Toronto. In back (left to right): Joseph's granddaughter's husband, Tomer; great-grandson Ori, on Tomer's shoulders; granddaughter, Liat, holding great-granddaughter, Noa; Joseph's daughter, Eve; Joseph; and his son-in-law, Rob. In front, Joseph's wife, Schulamit. 2015.

1 Waiting for the ballet. From left to right: Joseph's wife, Schulamit; Joseph's son-in-law, Rob; Joseph's daughter, Eve; and Joseph. Toronto, 2015.

2 Joseph with his wife, Schulamit; granddaughter, Liat; Liat's husband, Tomer; and Joseph's great-grandchildren Ori (left) and Noa (right). Rishon LeZion, Israel, 2016.

3 Joseph with his great-grandson Israel Reign Knights. Toronto, 2017.

Index

French Forces of the Interior
(FFI), 85
France. *See also* Vichy (France); antisemitism, xxiii, xxviii, 88–89;
deportations, xxiv, xxv; fifth
column, 37; under German oc-
cupation, xxii–xxvi, xxvii–xxix,
48, 55, 100; German retreat,
75–76; German surrender, xxxiii
Franco, Francisco, 6
Francs-Tireurs et Partisans (FTP),
xxx, xxxi, 78, 88
Free French Forces, xxxi, 83–84
free zone (France). *See* Vichy
(France)
French Communist Party, xxx–xxxi,
xxxii, 70, 77
French Foreign Legion (FFL), 52, 57
French Resistance, xxix–xxxiii, 63,
69, 77–92
French State *(l'État français),* xxii,
xxviii, xxix. *See also* Vichy
(France)
Freud, Jacob, xvi
Freud, Sigmund, xvi
Frisch, Alfred, 59, 62, 67–68, 69, 70,
72–73, 75
Frisch, Lilian, 59, 67–68, 69, 72–73,
75
Fromm, Bella, xviii
FTP (Francs-Tireurs et Partisans),
xxx, xxxi, 78, 88
FTP Company 2202, 78
FTP-MOI units, xxxi, xxxii
Gaza Strip, 139
gendarmes, xxiii, 45, 46, 52, 53, 67

Geneva Conventions, 85
Gerlier, Pierre-Marie, xxvi
German forces: in France, 36–37,
41–42; in retreat, 91
German prisoners, 80–81
German Reich, xvi
Germany: attack on Western
Front, 33; collapse, 99; invasion
of Belgium, xxi; invasion/oc-
cupation of France, xxii–xxiii;
Jewish population pre-war, xv,
xvii; Kristallnacht, xviii–xix,
16, 18, 19; under Nazi control,
xvii–xviii; pre-war, 3–4; retreat
from Belgium, 100; retreat from
France, 75–76; surrender, xxxiii,
102
Gestapo, 10, 64–65, 68, 72, 75
Glasberg, Alexandre, xxvi–xxvii,
xlii, 57, 64, 64n2
Gnome et Rhône (manufacturer),
71
Gourfinkel, Nina, xxvi, 64n2
grandfather, 6, 7–8
Grunbaum, Harry, 30
Gurs internment camp, xxvi
Habima Theatre (Israel), 117
hachsharah (training program), 13
Hadera (Israel), 115, 125
Haganah, 122, 123, 124, 125, 128, 138
Haifa (Israel), 107–8, 148
Haït, Ninon, 64n2
Hashomer Hatzair, 100, 101, 105, 116
Hausman, Bobbie, 30
Hausman, Manny, 30
Hebron (Israel), 136